RISC-V Programming Gu...

Getting Started with the RISC-V Microcontroller and C/C++
First Edition
Sarful Hassan

Preface

The **RISC-V Programming Guide: Getting Started with the RISC-V Microcontroller and C/C++** is designed to introduce readers to the world of RISC-V microcontroller programming, specifically with the SiFive HiFive1 Rev B development board. Whether you are a hobbyist, a student, or a professional developer, this book provides the foundational knowledge and practical skills needed to begin developing applications in the RISC-V ecosystem.

Who This Book Is For

This book is intended for:

- Engineers and developers interested in RISC-V programming.
- Students learning microcontroller programming and embedded systems.
- Makers and hobbyists looking to explore the capabilities of the SiFive HiFive1 Rev B.
- Professionals transitioning from traditional microcontrollers (like ARM or AVR) to RISC-V.

Basic familiarity with programming in C or C++ is assumed. No prior experience with RISC-V microcontrollers is required.

How This Book Is Organized

- **Chapter 1:** Provides a high-level introduction to RISC-V microcontrollers, their architecture, and their ecosystem.
- **Chapters 2–4:** Focus on setting up your development environment and foundational programming concepts like constants, variables, and data types.
- **Chapters 5–10:** Cover input/output programming, including digital, analog, and advanced I/O techniques.
- **Chapters 11–16:** Dive deeper into programming structures, operators, and functions in C tailored to microcontrollers.

- **Chapters 17–21:** Explore advanced topics such as power management, memory usage, communication protocols, and IoT applications with Wi-Fi.

What Was Left Out

Given the broad scope of RISC-V and microcontroller programming, this book focuses specifically on:

- The SiFive HiFive1 Rev B board.
- Programming in C and C++.

Advanced topics like real-time operating systems (RTOS), hardware debugging, or extensive third-party libraries are not covered in detail. These are planned for future editions or companion books.

Code Style (About the Code)

All code examples are written in standard C with an emphasis on clarity and simplicity.

- Code snippets are formatted for readability and tested on the HiFive1 Rev B board.
- Comments and documentation are included to help explain functionality.

Where necessary, the code adheres to modern embedded programming practices, ensuring compatibility and ease of use.

Release Notes

- This **First Edition** focuses on the HiFive1 Rev B. Future updates may include additional boards and enhanced features as the RISC-V ecosystem evolves.
- Errata and updates will be published on **mechatronicslab.net** as they become available.

Notes on the First Edition

This edition marks the first in a series dedicated to RISC-V programming. Feedback from readers is invaluable to improving the quality and scope of future editions.

MechatronicsLAB Online Learning

For additional resources, updates, and learning materials, visit:

- **Website:** mechatronicslab.net
- **Email:** mechatronicslab@gmail.com

We encourage readers to reach out with questions, suggestions, or feedback.

Acknowledgments for the First Edition

This book would not have been possible without the support of the following individuals and organizations:

- The team at SiFive for their contributions to the RISC-V ecosystem.
- The vibrant online RISC-V community for their insights and discussions.
- My colleagues and students at MechatronicsLAB who provided valuable feedback during the writing process.

Copyright (MechatronicsLAB)

Disclaimer

The information in this book is provided "as is." While every effort has been made to ensure accuracy, the author and publisher assume no responsibility for errors, omissions, or any damages resulting from the use of the material in this book. Readers are encouraged to test all code examples and use them at their own risk.

Table of Contents

Introduction to RISC-V Microcontrollers

What is RISC-V?

RISC-V is an open-standard Instruction Set Architecture (ISA) based on Reduced Instruction Set Computing (RISC) principles. Unlike proprietary ISAs like ARM or x86, RISC-V is free and open for anyone to use, modify, and implement without licensing fees or royalties. This openness has made RISC-V a catalyst for innovation, enabling the development of cost-effective, customizable processors and microcontrollers.

Key Features of RISC-V:

- Modular design allows for a tailored approach, with optional extensions for specific use cases.
- Scalable across applications, from simple microcontrollers to high-performance computing.
- Backed by an active open-source community, ensuring rapid development and transparency.

History and Significance of RISC-V

RISC-V was created in 2010 at the University of California, Berkeley, led by Krste Asanović and David Patterson. It emerged as a response to the limitations of proprietary ISAs, which often hindered innovation due to high costs and restrictive licensing agreements.

Significance:

- **Academic Research**: Provides a free platform for students and researchers to experiment and innovate.
- **Industrial Impact**: Enables startups and established companies to develop hardware without vendor lock-in.
- **Global Adoption**: The flexibility and cost-effectiveness of RISC-V have led to its adoption in IoT, consumer electronics, and robotics.

Advantages of Open-Source Hardware

Open-source hardware, exemplified by RISC-V, is reshaping the tech industry.

Comparison with Proprietary Architectures

Aspect	Proprietary ISAs (e.g., ARM)	Open-Source ISAs (e.g., RISC-V)
Licensing	Requires royalties and fees	Free and open
Customizability	Limited by vendor agreements	Fully customizable
Ecosystem Control	Vendor-driven	Community-driven
Cost	Higher	Lower

Benefits of Open-Source Hardware:

1. **Cost Efficiency**: No royalties or licensing fees reduce development costs.
2. **Transparency**: Access to source code ensures no hidden vulnerabilities.
3. **Customizability**: Developers can modify the ISA to optimize performance for specific applications.
4. **Collaboration**: Open-source communities encourage knowledge sharing and rapid problem-solving.
5. **Vendor Independence**: Avoids being tied to a single supplier, providing greater flexibility.

The Role of Microcontrollers
Microcontrollers vs. Microprocessors

Aspect	Microcontrollers (MCUs)	Microprocessors (MPUs)
Integration	Processor, memory, peripherals	Processor only
Focus	Single-task embedded applications	High-performance multitasking
Memory	On-chip	External
Power Consumption	Low	High
Applications	IoT, automation, consumer devices	Desktops, laptops, and servers

Microcontrollers (MCUs) are compact integrated circuits designed for specific tasks in embedded systems. They include memory, processing power, and peripherals on a single chip.

Embedded Systems in Everyday Applications
Microcontrollers power many embedded systems we use daily, such as:

- **Consumer Electronics**: Smart TVs, washing machines, and wearables.
- **Industrial Automation**: Robotic arms, conveyor systems, and sensors.
- **Automotive**: Engine control units, ABS systems, and infotainment devices.

Why Choose RISC-V Microcontrollers?
Comparison with ARM and AVR Architectures

Feature	RISC-V	ARM Cortex-M	AVR
ISA	Open-source	Proprietary	Legacy RISC
Licensing	Free	Requires royalties	No royalties (fixed ISA)
Scalability	Highly scalable	Fixed scalability tiers	Limited
Ecosystem Control	Community-driven	Vendor-driven	Limited community support

Benefits of RISC-V for IoT and Robotics

1. **Customizability**: RISC-V microcontrollers can be tailored to specific tasks, optimizing performance and power consumption.
2. **Cost Efficiency**: Open-source hardware reduces production costs, making RISC-V ideal for cost-sensitive applications like IoT devices.
3. **Scalability**: Suitable for diverse applications, from simple sensors to advanced robotic systems.

Why RISC-V Excels:

- **IoT Applications**: Low-power, customizable features make RISC-V MCUs perfect for battery-powered devices.
- **Robotics**: Real-time processing capabilities support precise control and sensor integration.

Use Cases of RISC-V Microcontrollers
Examples in IoT, Consumer Electronics, and Automation

- **IoT**: Smart home devices, such as thermostats and security cameras, benefit from RISC-V's low-power design and connectivity options.
- **Consumer Electronics**: Wearables like fitness trackers use RISC-V for data processing and Bluetooth communication.
- **Automation**: Industrial robots and controllers leverage RISC-V for real-time performance and scalability.

Overview of SiFive HiFive1 Rev B

The HiFive1 Rev B is a popular development board featuring a RISC-V microcontroller.

Key Features and Specifications:

- **Microcontroller**: SiFive FE310-G002 (RV32IMAC)
- **Clock Speed**: Up to 320 MHz
- **Memory**: 16 KB instruction cache, 8 KB SRAM
- **GPIO Pins**: 19 digital I/O pins, 9 PWM outputs
- **Connectivity**: USB, JTAG, and SPI

Applications and Use Cases:

- Ideal for learning RISC-V programming and experimenting with embedded systems.
- Used in IoT prototypes, robotics, and low-power sensor networks.

Microcontroller Basics

Components of a Microcontroller

Microcontrollers are highly integrated devices that combine the essential components needed to control embedded systems. These components work together to process data, control devices, and communicate with the outside world.

Central Processing Unit (CPU)

- **Role**: The brain of the microcontroller, responsible for executing program instructions.
- **Features**:
    - Implements an Instruction Set Architecture (ISA) such as RISC-V.
    - Includes an Arithmetic Logic Unit (ALU) for calculations and logic operations.
    - Manages control signals for the microcontroller's peripherals.

Memory

Microcontrollers typically include three types of memory:

- **Flash Memory**: Non-volatile storage for program code. Retains data when powered off.
- **SRAM (Static RAM)**: Volatile memory used for temporary storage during program execution, such as variables and stack data.
- **EEPROM** (optional): Non-volatile memory for storing configuration data or parameters that need to persist across power cycles.

General Purpose Input/Output (GPIO)

- **Functionality**: GPIO pins enable the microcontroller to interact with external devices, such as sensors, LEDs, or buttons.
- **Modes**:
    - Input: Reads signals from external devices.
    - Output: Sends signals to control devices like motors or relays.

- **Features**: Configurable pull-up or pull-down resistors for stability and multi-function support for alternate peripheral connections.

Peripherals

Peripherals extend the microcontroller's capabilities beyond basic computation. Examples include:

- **Timers**: Measure time intervals, generate delays, or produce PWM signals.
- **ADC (Analog-to-Digital Converter)**: Converts analog sensor signals to digital data for processing.
- **UART, I2C, SPI**: Communication protocols for interfacing with external devices.

Understanding Embedded Systems
What are Embedded Systems?

Embedded systems are dedicated computing systems designed to perform specific tasks within larger systems. They integrate hardware and software optimized for efficiency and reliability.

Examples of Embedded Systems

- **Automotive**: Engine control units, airbag systems, and infotainment devices.
- **Consumer Electronics**: Washing machines, microwave ovens, and wearable devices.
- **Industrial Automation**: Temperature controllers, robotic arms, and conveyor systems.

Role of Microcontrollers in Modern Devices

Microcontrollers are the backbone of embedded systems, handling tasks such as:

1. **Sensor Data Processing**: Reading and interpreting input signals.
2. **Control Logic Execution**: Making decisions based on sensor inputs and predefined conditions.
3. **Actuator Control**: Sending output signals to drive motors, LEDs, or other devices.

How Microcontrollers Work in Real-World Applications
From Sensors to Actuators: A Typical Workflow
1. **Input Stage (Sensors)**:
    o   Microcontrollers read data from sensors, such as temperature, pressure, or motion sensors, via ADC or GPIO pins.
2. **Processing Stage**:
    o   The CPU processes the input data using algorithms or logic stored in the program memory.
    o   Decisions are made based on conditions, such as exceeding a threshold or responding to an event.
3. **Output Stage (Actuators)**:
    o   Control signals are sent to actuators like motors, LEDs, or relays.
    o   For example, turning on a cooling fan when a temperature sensor detects excessive heat.

Example: A smart thermostat reads room temperature, compares it to a set value, and turns on the HVAC system if needed.

Comparison of RISC-V with Other Architectures

Feature	RISC-V	ARM Cortex-M	AVR
ISA	Open-source, modular	Proprietary, efficient	Proprietary, fixed
Scalability	Highly scalable	Multiple tiers available	Limited
Licensing	No royalties	Requires licensing fees	No licensing fees
Performance	Optimized for various tasks	Optimized for efficiency	Moderate for simple tasks
Ecosystem	Community-driven	Vendor-driven	Smaller ecosystem

Performance and Cost-Effectiveness:

- RISC-V offers excellent scalability, allowing developers to create microcontrollers tailored to their needs.
- Its open-source nature eliminates licensing costs, making it more affordable for budget-conscious applications.
- Compared to ARM, RISC-V provides similar performance while offering greater design flexibility.

Flexibility for Developers:

RISC-V's modular ISA enables custom instruction sets, reducing power consumption and die size for specific applications like IoT sensors and robotics.

HiFive1 Rev B Pinout and Features

HiFive1 Rev B Overview

The HiFive1 Rev B is a development board designed by SiFive for RISC-V programming and prototyping. It features the SiFive FE310-G002 microcontroller.

Key Features

- **Clock Speed**: Up to 320 MHz.
- **Memory**: 16 KB instruction cache, 8 KB SRAM.
- **GPIO Pins**: 19 digital I/O pins with multi-function support.
- **Peripherals**: SPI, I2C, PWM, UART.
- **Connectivity**: USB for programming and debugging.

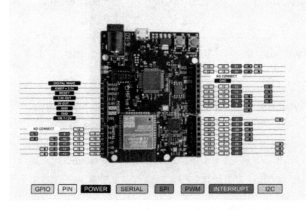

Pinout Table

Pin	Function	Description
GPIO0-GPIO17	Digital I/O, PWM, UART, SPI	General-purpose I/O pins
A0-A3	Analog inputs	ADC for reading sensor signals
VIN	Power input	Supplies voltage to the board
GND	Ground	Common ground
RESET	Reset input	Resets the microcontroller

Voltage Levels and Alternate Functions

- **GPIO Voltage Levels**: Operates at 3.3V logic levels.
- **Alternate Functions**: Many GPIO pins double as communication or peripheral interfaces, such as UART (serial communication) or SPI (serial peripherals).

RISC-V Architecture Overview

Core Features of RISC-V

RISC-V is a modern implementation of the Reduced Instruction Set Computing (RISC) philosophy. Its architecture prioritizes simplicity, efficiency, and scalability, making it highly adaptable for various applications, from microcontrollers to supercomputers.

Principles of Reduced Instruction Set Computing (RISC)

- **Simplified Instruction Set**: RISC architectures use fewer, more streamlined instructions that can execute in a single clock cycle, improving efficiency.
- **Load/Store Architecture**: Arithmetic and logic operations are performed only on registers, while memory access is limited to specific instructions, reducing complexity.

- **Uniform Instruction Format**: Fixed-length instructions simplify decoding and pipelining in hardware, enhancing performance.

Modular Design of RISC-V ISA

RISC-V's architecture is inherently modular, allowing developers to select only the features they need. This approach leads to optimized designs tailored for specific use cases.

- **Base ISA**: The foundational instruction set, required for all RISC-V implementations.
- **Extensions**: Optional additions that enhance functionality, such as floating-point operations or atomic instructions.

Instruction Set Architecture (ISA)
Base Integer Set: RV32I

The RV32I base instruction set is the core of RISC-V's design, providing 32-bit instructions for basic integer operations.

- **Arithmetic Operations**: Add, subtract, shift, and logical operations.
- **Control Flow**: Branching and jumping instructions for program flow.
- **Memory Access**: Load and store operations for interacting with memory.

Example RV32I Instructions:

- ADD rd, rs1, rs2: Adds the values in registers rs1 and rs2, storing the result in rd.
- LW rd, offset(rs1): Loads a word from memory at the address specified by rs1 + offset into rd.

Common Extensions

1. **M (Multiplication/Division)**:
   - Adds hardware support for multiply and divide operations, critical for numerical applications like digital signal processing.
   - Example: MUL rd, rs1, rs2 (Multiplies values in rs1 and rs2, stores the result in rd).

2. **C (Compressed Instructions)**:
   - Introduces 16-bit instructions to reduce code size, ideal for memory-constrained environments like IoT devices.

- o Example: C.ADDI (Compressed version of ADDI instruction).
3. **F and D (Floating-Point)**:
    - o Enables single (F) and double (D) precision floating-point calculations for scientific and graphical applications.

Registers and Memory Layout
General-Purpose Registers and Memory Addressing
RISC-V features 32 general-purpose registers (x0 to x31), each 32 or 64 bits wide depending on the ISA.

- **x0**: Always holds the value 0.
- **x1 (ra)**: Return address register for function calls.
- **x2 (sp)**: Stack pointer for managing local variables and function calls.
- **x10-x17 (a0-a7)**: Used for passing arguments to functions and returning results.

RISC-V Memory Addressing Modes
1. **Base + Offset**: The effective address is calculated as base register + offset.
    - o Example: LW x5, 4(x10) (Loads a word from memory at address x10 + 4 into x5).
2. **PC-Relative Addressing**: Useful for branching and jumping instructions, where the target address is relative to the current program counter (PC).
3. **Register-Indirect Addressing**: Allows dynamic memory access by specifying the address in a register.

Little-Endian Format and Addressing Schemes
RISC-V uses little-endian memory representation, where the least significant byte is stored at the lowest memory address. This format simplifies interoperability with modern systems and peripherals.

SiFive E31 Core in HiFive1 Rev B
Overview of the Core Architecture
The SiFive E31 is a high-performance, 32-bit RISC-V core designed for embedded systems. It is implemented in the HiFive1 Rev B development board, providing an accessible platform for learning and prototyping.

Key Features of the E31 Core:
- **RV32IMAC ISA**: Implements the base integer set (RV32I) along with the M (multiplication), A (atomic), and C (compressed) extensions.
- **Pipeline**: Features a 5-stage in-order pipeline for efficient instruction execution.
- **Interrupt Controller**: Supports advanced interrupt handling for real-time applications.

Customization and Performance Features
- **Custom Instructions**: Developers can add custom instructions to optimize performance for specific tasks.
- **Low Power Consumption**: Designed with energy-efficient features, making it suitable for IoT and wearable devices.
- **Cache System**: Includes a 16 KB instruction cache, reducing memory access latency.

RISC-V Microcontroller Ecosystem

Overview of Popular RISC-V Boards
The growing RISC-V ecosystem includes several development boards designed for prototyping, learning, and deploying embedded applications. Below are three popular RISC-V boards:

1. SiFive HiFive1 Rev B
- **Processor**: SiFive FE310-G002 (RV32IMAC ISA).
- **Clock Speed**: Up to 320 MHz.
- **Memory**: 16 KB instruction cache, 8 KB SRAM.
- **Features**:
  - 19 GPIO pins.
  - SPI, I2C, PWM, and UART peripherals.
  - Arduino-compatible headers for easy prototyping.
- **Applications**: IoT devices, education, and general-purpose embedded systems.

2. ESP32-C3
- **Processor**: 32-bit RISC-V core with integrated Wi-Fi and Bluetooth Low Energy (BLE).
- **Clock Speed**: Up to 160 MHz.
- **Features**:

- 12-bit ADC, UART, SPI, and I2C interfaces.
- On-chip security features like secure boot and hardware cryptography.
- **Applications**: IoT devices requiring wireless connectivity, such as smart home and wearables.

3. GD32VF103

- **Processor**: Bumblebee RISC-V core (RV32IMAC ISA).
- **Clock Speed**: Up to 108 MHz.
- **Features**:
  - Rich peripheral set, including timers, ADC, DAC, UART, SPI, and I2C.
  - Low power consumption with advanced interrupt handling.
- **Applications**: Industrial automation, robotics, and low-power consumer electronics.

Development Tools and Resources

A robust set of tools and resources supports RISC-V development, making it accessible for beginners and professionals alike.

Freedom Studio

- SiFive's Eclipse-based IDE designed for RISC-V development.
- Provides integrated debugging, code editing, and project management.
- Preconfigured toolchains for boards like the HiFive1 Rev B.

PlatformIO

- A cross-platform IDE with RISC-V support via VS Code.
- Features include library management, debugging, and firmware uploading.

GCC Toolchain

- The GNU Compiler Collection supports RISC-V development with compilers, linkers, and debuggers.
- Includes tools like riscv64-unknown-elf-gcc for bare-metal development and gdb for debugging.

Open-Source Communities and Documentation

- **RISC-V International**: Maintains standards, specifications, and documentation.

- **GitHub Repositories**: Hosts open-source projects, peripheral libraries, and tutorials. Examples include SiFive's official repositories and PlatformIO projects.
- **Forums and Groups**: Platforms like Stack Overflow, RISC-V forums, and Discord communities provide developer support and discussions.

Popular IDEs and Toolchains for RISC-V
VS Code with PlatformIO
- **Features**:
    1. Simplified project setup and board selection.
    2. Integrated terminal for toolchain commands.
    3. Library manager for accessing open-source code.
- **Setup**:
    1. Install VS Code.
    2. Add the PlatformIO extension.
    3. Create a new project and select your RISC-V board.

Eclipse-Based Freedom Studio
- **Features**:
    o Preconfigured for SiFive RISC-V cores.
    o Integrated debugging tools with OpenOCD support.
- **Use Cases**: Ideal for HiFive1 Rev B and other SiFive-based boards.

SiFive Freedom SDK
- A software development kit specifically for SiFive RISC-V boards.
- **Features**:
    o Includes example libraries for GPIO, SPI, UART, and more.
    o Simplifies peripheral initialization and low-level programming.

Installing and Setting Up the SDK
Clone the SDK repository:

```
git clone https://github.com/sifive/freedom-e-sdk.git
cd freedom-e-sdk
```

Build the toolchain and flash utilities:

make tools

Flash an example program:

```
make BOARD=hiFive1-revb PROGRAM=gpio PORT=/dev/ttyUSB0 upload
```

Example Libraries and Support for HiFive1 Rev B
- **GPIO Library**: Simplifies pin configuration and control.
- **SPI and I2C Libraries**: For communication with external devices.
- **Timer Library**: For generating delays and measuring time intervals.

Choosing the Right RISC-V Development Board
When selecting a RISC-V development board, consider the following factors:
1. **Application Requirements**
   - Does the board have the necessary peripherals (e.g., ADC, PWM, communication interfaces) for your project?
   - Example: ESP32-C3 for IoT projects requiring wireless connectivity.
2. **Performance Needs**
   - Choose a board with sufficient processing power and memory.
   - Example: HiFive1 Rev B for general-purpose embedded systems.
3. **Community and Documentation**
   - Boards like HiFive1 Rev B benefit from extensive documentation and community support.
4. **Budget Constraints**
   - Sipeed Longan Nano and GD32VF103 are affordable options for budget-conscious developers.
5. **Ease of Use** Beginners may prefer boards with Arduino

Setting Up the Development Environment

Installing Tools for RISC-V Development

To develop for RISC-V microcontrollers, you'll need the appropriate toolchains and development environments. This section covers the essential steps for setting up tools like PlatformIO and Freedom Studio.

PlatformIO within Visual Studio Code
PlatformIO is a powerful extension for Visual Studio Code that simplifies RISC-V development.

1. **Install Visual Studio Code**
   o Download and install VS Code.
2. **Add the PlatformIO Extension**
   o Open VS Code, navigate to the Extensions Marketplace, and search for "PlatformIO IDE."
   o Click **Install** to add PlatformIO to your environment.
3. **Create a New RISC-V Project**
   o Click on the **PlatformIO Home** icon in the bottom toolbar.
   o Select **New Project**, choose your board (e.g., SiFive HiFive1 Rev B), and specify the project directory.
   o PlatformIO will automatically download the required frameworks and libraries for the selected board.

Configuring Freedom Studio for HiFive1 Rev B
Freedom Studio is SiFive's Eclipse-based IDE tailored for RISC-V development.

1. **Download and Install Freedom Studio**
   o Visit the Freedom Studio website and download the installer for your operating system.
   o Install the software and open the IDE.
2. **Set Up a New Project**
   o Select **File > New > Freedom E SDK Project**.
   o Choose **HiFive1 Rev B** as your target board.
   o Import example programs or start with a blank project.

3. **Configure the Toolchain**
   - ○ Freedom Studio comes preconfigured with the RISC-V GNU toolchain. Verify the toolchain path in **Window > Preferences > C/C++ > Build > Environment**.

Connecting and Testing the HiFive1 Rev B

Setting Up Hardware and Drivers

1. **Connect the Board**
   - ○ Use a micro-USB cable to connect the HiFive1 Rev B to your computer.
   - ○ Ensure the board is powered on (the power LED should light up).
2. **Install Drivers**
   - ○ On Windows: Install FTDI drivers if prompted.
   - ○ On Linux/Mac: Ensure that the user has permissions to access the serial port (e.g., /dev/ttyUSB0).

Writing and Uploading Your First "Hello, World!" Program
The "Hello, World!" program demonstrates the basics of configuring and running a RISC-V application.

Write the Code

```c
#include <stdio.h>

int main() {
    printf("Hello, World!\n");
    while (1);
    return 0;
}
```

1. **Compile the Program**
   - ○ If using PlatformIO: Save the code in your project's src folder.
   - ○ Click **Build** in the PlatformIO toolbar.
2. **Upload the Program**
   - ○ Use the **Upload** button in PlatformIO to flash the program to the HiFive1 Rev B.
   - ○ If using Freedom Studio, select **Run > Debug As > Freedom E SDK Debug** to upload and execute.

3. **View Output**
   - Open a serial terminal (e.g., PlatformIO's terminal or `minicom`) to see the "Hello, World!" message.

Overview of Debugging with JTAG and OpenOCD

Debugging Basics for the HiFive1 Rev B
Debugging allows developers to analyze code behavior, identify issues, and optimize performance. The HiFive1 Rev B supports debugging via JTAG, a hardware debugging interface.

Using JTAG and OpenOCD for Troubleshooting

1. **Install OpenOCD**

On Linux:

```
sudo apt install openocd
```

   - On Windows: Download OpenOCD binaries from the official site or package manager (e.g., Chocolatey).
2. **Connect via JTAG**
   - Connect the HiFive1 Rev B's JTAG header to your computer using an FTDI or similar JTAG adapter.
1. **Start OpenOCD**

Run OpenOCD with the correct configuration files:

```
openocd -f board/sifive-hifive1-revb.cfg
```

4. **Debug with GDB**

Start GDB with the compiled firmware:

```
riscv64-unknown-elf-gdb firmware.elf
```

Connect GDB to OpenOCD:

```
target remote localhost:3333
```

- Set breakpoints, inspect variables, and step through the code.

Troubleshooting Common Setup Issues

Driver Installation Problems

1. **Issue**: The board is not recognized.
   - **Solution**: Ensure FTDI or USB drivers are installed. Check for the correct serial port in the device manager (Windows) or `/dev/` directory (Linux/Mac).
2. **Issue**: Permissions error on Linux.

Solution: Add your user to the `dialout` group:

```
sudo usermod -aG dialout $USER
```

- Log out and back in for changes to take effect.

Resolving Communication Errors with the Board

1. **Issue**: Serial terminal shows no output.
   - **Solution**: Verify the baud rate matches the board's configuration (e.g., 115200).
2. **Issue**: Firmware upload fails.
   - **Solution**:
     - Check the connection and ensure the board is powered.
     - Restart the board and retry the upload process.

   - compatibility or well-integrated IDEs.

Constants and Variables in C for RISC-V Microcontrollers

Chapter Overview

In embedded programming with RISC-V microcontrollers, constants and variables are foundational elements for managing data. Constants store unchanging values, while variables hold data that can be modified as the program runs. Proper management of constants and variables in code helps improve readability, efficiency, and stability, which are crucial for the constrained environments of embedded systems. This chapter will guide you through the syntax, usage, and best practices for constants and variables, and provide a practical project to demonstrate these concepts in action.

Chapter Goal

- Understand the difference between constants and variables and their specific roles in RISC-V programming.
- Learn the syntax for declaring, initializing, and modifying constants and variables.
- Apply constants and variables in a practical project that demonstrates optimal code efficiency and readability.

Rules

- **Use Constants for Fixed Values**: Define constant values for parameters that should not change, like mathematical constants or hardware configurations.
- **Initialize Variables Properly**: Assign initial values to variables when declaring them to avoid errors or undefined behaviors.
- **Choose the Appropriate Data Type**: Select data types based on the expected range of values for efficient memory use.
- **Use Descriptive Names**: Naming variables and constants clearly improves code readability.

Brief Introduction to Constants and Variables

In C programming, variables represent storage locations in memory where data can be stored, retrieved, and modified. Constants, on the other hand, are fixed values that remain unchanged throughout the program. In embedded programming, where memory and processing power are limited, using constants and variables effectively can help improve program efficiency and prevent errors.

Syntax Table

Serial No	Topic	Syntax	Simple Example
1	Variable Declaration	`type variableName;`	`int counter;`
2	Variable Initialization	`type variableName = value;`	`float voltage = 5.0;`
3	Constant Declaration	`const type constName = value;`	`const int MAX = 10;`
4	Constant with #define	`#define CONST_NAME value`	`#define PI 3.14159`
5	Modifying Variable Value	`variableName = newValue;`	`counter = 10;`

Detailed Breakdown for Each Command

1. Variable Declaration

What is Variable Declaration?

Declaring a variable in C allocates a storage location in memory for it and assigns it a specific data type. This enables the program to store and manage data that may change during execution.

Use Purpose

- **Store Dynamic Data**: Variables store values that can change throughout the program, such as counters or sensor readings.
- **Enable Calculations**: Variables facilitate dynamic calculations by holding intermediate or changing values.

Syntax

```
type variableName;
```

Syntax Explanation

- **type**: Defines the data type, such as int, float, or char, which determines the kind of data the variable will store.
- **variableName**: The name of the variable, following C's naming conventions (start with a letter or underscore and avoid spaces or special characters).

Simple Code Example

```
int counter;
```

Code Example Explanation

- This line declares an integer variable named counter that can store integer values and be modified as needed in the program.

Notes

- Choose descriptive names to clarify each variable's purpose.
- Declare variables close to their first use to improve readability.

Warnings

- Declaring variables without initializing them may result in unpredictable values stored in memory.

2. Variable Initialization

What is Variable Initialization?
Initializing a variable assigns it a starting value at the time of declaration. This ensures the variable has a defined, predictable value from the beginning, avoiding undefined states.

Use Purpose

- **Ensure Consistent Initial State**: Initialization prepares the variable for immediate use with a known value.
- **Avoid Unpredictable Values**: Starting with a defined value helps prevent errors in calculations or logic.

Syntax

```
type variableName = value;
```

Syntax Explanation

- **type**: Defines the data type of the variable.
- **variableName**: The name of the variable.
- **value**: The initial value assigned to the variable, matching the data type.

Simple Code Example

```
float voltage = 5.0;
```

Code Example Explanation

- This initializes a float variable named voltage with an initial value of 5.0.

Notes

- Initialization is particularly helpful for counters or status flags.

- Initialize variables as close to their first use as possible for better code organization.

---

3. Constant Declaration

What is Constant Declaration?
A constant declaration defines a read-only variable, meaning its value cannot be modified after it is assigned. Constants are useful for fixed values such as configuration settings, mathematical constants, or limits.

Use Purpose

- **Ensure Fixed Values**: Constants prevent accidental changes to critical values.
- **Improve Code Clarity**: Assigning descriptive names to fixed values makes code easier to understand.

Syntax
```
const type constName = value;
```
Syntax Explanation

- **const**: Keyword that makes the variable read-only.
- **type**: Defines the data type of the constant.
- **constName**: The name of the constant, often written in uppercase to indicate its fixed nature.
- **value**: The initial and final value of the constant.

Simple Code Example
```
const int MAX_COUNT = 10;
```

Code Example Explanation

- This defines MAX_COUNT as a constant integer with a value of 10. Once assigned, MAX_COUNT cannot be modified.

Notes

- Constants are often declared at the beginning of the program for easy access and clarity.
- Using constants helps avoid "magic numbers" in code, improving maintainability.

---

4. Constant with #define

What is Constant with #define?
Using #define creates a symbolic constant that the compiler replaces with the specified value during compile time. It's often used for global values that don't require memory allocation.

Use Purpose

- **Memory Efficient**: #define constants do not occupy memory.
- **Global Accessibility**: Values defined with #define are accessible throughout the program.

Syntax
```
#define CONST_NAME value
```

Syntax Explanation

- **#define**: Preprocessor directive used to define a constant.
- **CONST_NAME**: Typically uppercase to indicate it's a constant.
- **value**: The assigned value, which replaces every occurrence of CONST_NAME during compile time.

Simple Code Example
```
#define PI 3.14159
```

Code Example Explanation

- Defines PI with the value 3.14159, replacing every instance of PI in the code with 3.14159 during compilation.

Notes

- #define constants do not require memory, making them efficient for repetitive values.
- Use for constants required across multiple files or modules.

---

5. Modifying Variable Value

What is Modifying Variable Value?
Modifying a variable's value allows updating its content dynamically, which is essential for tasks involving counters, flags, or calculations.

Use Purpose

- **Track Changes**: Variables can store values that update based on the program's needs.
- **Hold Intermediate Results**: Variables can store results temporarily for calculations and comparisons.

Syntax

```
variableName = newValue;
```

Syntax Explanation

- **variableName**: The variable to be updated.
- **newValue**: The new value to assign to the variable, matching the variable's data type.

Simple Code Example

```
counter = 10;
```

Code Example Explanation

- This assigns a new value of 10 to the variable counter, updating its content.

Notes
- Variables in loops or conditionals often get updated to reflect changing states or conditions.
Warnings

- Ensure the new value is within the variable's data type range to avoid errors.

Relevant Project Section

Project Name
LED Blinking with Adjustable Interval

Project Goal
Use constants and variables to control the blink rate of an LED on a RISC-V microcontroller. The LED blink interval will be determined by a constant, while a variable will manage the LED's on/off state.

RISC-V Development Environment
We will use **PlatformIO** within **Visual Studio Code** for this project. PlatformIO offers tools for building, uploading, and debugging code for RISC-V microcontrollers.

RISC-V Microcontroller
This example uses the **SiFive HiFive1 Rev B** microcontroller, based on the SiFive Freedom E310, a RISC-V core known for efficient IoT applications.

Requirement Components

- **SiFive HiFive1 Rev B RISC-V Microcontroller**
- **LED** connected to a GPIO output pin

Component Connection Table

Component	RISC-V Pin	Additional Notes
LED	GPIO Pin19	Controlled by software

Connection Analysis
The LED is connected to a GPIO pin on the HiFive1 Rev B, toggling on and off based on a timing interval set by a constant. The LED

state (on or off) is stored in a variable and modified based on timing logic.

Program Software Setup

1. Open **Visual Studio Code** with PlatformIO.
2. Create a new PlatformIO project and select **SiFive HiFive1 Rev B** as the board.
3. Define constants for the LED's blink interval and initialize the LED control variable.
4. Write code to toggle the LED state based on the defined interval.

Project Code

```c
#include <stdint.h>

// Define the pin number for the onboard LED
#define LED_PIN 19

// Define GPIO control registers based on your SDK
#define GPIO_DIR (*(volatile uint32_t*)0x10012000)  // GPIO direction
register
#define GPIO_OUT (*(volatile uint32_t*)0x10012004)  // GPIO output
register

const int BLINK_INTERVAL = 100000; // LED blink interval in cycles
int ledState = 0;                  // Variable to track LED state

// Function to configure the LED pin as an output
void setupLED() {
    GPIO_DIR |= (1 << LED_PIN);    // Set LED_PIN as output
    GPIO_OUT &= ~(1 << LED_PIN);   // Ensure LED is initially off
}

// Simple delay function using a busy-wait loop
void delay(int interval) {
    for (volatile int i = 0; i < interval; i++); // Waste cycles for
delay
}

int main() {
    setupLED(); // Initialize LED

    while (1) {
        if (ledState) {
            GPIO_OUT &= ~(1 << LED_PIN); // Turn off LED
        } else {
            GPIO_OUT |= (1 << LED_PIN);  // Turn on LED
        }
```

```
        ledState = !ledState;   // Toggle LED state
        delay(BLINK_INTERVAL);  // Delay between toggles
    }

    return 0; // Program will never reach here
}
```

Save and Run

1. Save, compile, and upload the code to the SiFive HiFive1
   Rev B board using PlatformIO in Visual Studio Code.
2. Observe the LED toggling on and off, with the interval
   controlled by the BLINK_INTERVAL constant.

Check Output

- The LED should blink at a steady rate defined by the
  BLINK_INTERVAL constant, while the ledState variable
  manages its on/off state.

Data Types in C for RISC-V Microcontrollers

Chapter Overview
Data types are fundamental to programming, especially in embedded systems like RISC-V microcontrollers, where memory and processing power are limited. Data types define the kind of data a variable can hold (such as integers, characters, or floating-point numbers) and specify how much memory that data occupies. Using data types efficiently allows for optimal memory usage, helps prevent errors, and improves code readability and reliability. This chapter covers data types, including basic, derived, and user-defined types, with practical examples and guidelines.

Chapter Goal

- Understand the basic data types available in C programming for RISC-V microcontrollers.
- Learn to select the appropriate data types for specific applications to optimize memory usage.
- Implement a project demonstrating the use of various data types in a real-world scenario.

Rules

- **Choose Minimal Storage**: Use the smallest data type necessary to store the information (e.g., char for small integers).
- **Ensure Correct Data Range**: Choose data types that match the range of expected values to avoid overflow or underflow.
- **Use Floating Points Only When Necessary**: Floating-point operations consume more resources; use them sparingly.
- **Define Custom Types for Clarity**: When applicable, define custom types to improve code readability and maintainability.

Brief Introduction to Data Types

In C programming for embedded systems, data types categorize variables by the kind and size of data they store. Primitive data types like int, char, and float are used frequently, but derived types (arrays, pointers) and user-defined types (structs, unions) are also essential for complex data handling. In RISC-V microcontrollers, managing data types efficiently can greatly impact system performance and resource usage.

Syntax Table

Serial No	Topic	Syntax	Simple Example
1	Integer Declaration	`int varName;`	`int count;`
2	Character Declaration	`char varName;`	`char letter;`
3	Floating-Point Decl.	`float varName;`	`float temperature;`
4	Array Declaration	`type arrayName[size];`	`int numbers[5];`
5	Structure Declaration	`struct { type member; };`	`struct Student { int age; };`

Detailed Breakdown for Each Command
1. Integer Declaration
What is Integer Declaration?

An integer declaration creates a variable to store whole numbers. Integers are commonly used in embedded programming for counters, sensor values, or any whole-number data.

Use Purpose

- **Store Whole Numbers**: Ideal for counting and representing integer values.
- **Control Logic**: Frequently used in conditions and loops.

Syntax

```
int varName;
```

Syntax Explanation

- `int`: Specifies the variable as an integer type, usually requiring 2 or 4 bytes of memory depending on the platform.
- `varName`: The name of the integer variable.

Simple Code Example

```
int count;
```

Code Example Explanation

- Declares an integer variable `count`, which can hold whole-number values such as 10, -5, etc.

Notes

- The range of `int` varies based on the microcontroller's architecture (typically -32,768 to 32,767 for 16-bit, -2,147,483,648 to 2,147,483,647 for 32-bit).

Warnings

- Using an integer for values beyond its range will cause overflow.

---

2. Character Declaration

What is Character Declaration?

Character declarations define variables that can store single characters or small integers. Characters use 1 byte of memory and are commonly used for text data or small integer values.

Use Purpose

- **Store Single Characters**: Useful for text-based applications, such as displaying letters.
- **Small Integer Storage**: Can hold numbers from 0 to 255 (unsigned) or -128 to 127 (signed).

Syntax

```
char varName;
```

Syntax Explanation

- **char**: Specifies the variable as a character type.
- **varName**: The name of the character variable.

Simple Code Example

```
char letter;
```

Code Example Explanation

- Declares a char variable letter, which can store a character like 'A' or a small integer.

Notes

- char variables are frequently used in arrays to store strings.

Warnings

- Ensure character encoding is consistent if transferring between systems, as characters are represented in ASCII or Unicode.

---

3. Floating-Point Declaration

What is Floating-Point Declaration?
Floating-point declarations define variables to store decimal numbers, often used for precise measurements or fractional values in calculations.

Use Purpose

- **Store Decimal Values**: Useful for measurements, calculations, and any value requiring precision.
- **Handle Mathematical Operations**: Often used in applications requiring multiplication or division of fractional values.

Syntax

```
float varName;
```

Syntax Explanation

- **`float`**: Specifies the variable as a floating-point type, requiring 4 bytes of memory.
- **`varName`**: The name of the floating-point variable.

Simple Code Example

```
float temperature;
```

Code Example Explanation

- Declares a `float` variable `temperature`, which can hold decimal values such as `23.5` or `-2.8`.

Notes

- Floating-point operations are slower and more resource-intensive than integer operations.

---

4. Array Declaration

What is Array Declaration?
An array declaration creates a collection of elements of the same data type, allowing multiple values to be stored under a single variable name. Arrays are useful for grouping data, such as sensor readings or multiple characters.

Use Purpose

- **Store Multiple Values**: Allows storage of multiple elements of the same type.
- **Efficient Data Organization**: Ideal for managing data that can be processed in loops.

Syntax

```
type arrayName[size];
```

Syntax Explanation

- `type`: Specifies the data type of the elements.
- `arrayName`: The name of the array variable.
- `size`: Number of elements the array can hold.

Simple Code Example

```
int numbers[5];
```

Code Example Explanation

- Declares an array numbers with space for 5 integer elements.

Notes

- Arrays have a fixed size, which must be defined at declaration.

Warnings

- Accessing elements outside the array bounds will cause memory errors.

---

5. Structure Declaration
What is Structure Declaration?

A structure declaration groups different data types under a single variable, allowing related data to be managed together. Structures are useful for creating custom data types in embedded programming.

Use Purpose

- **Organize Related Data**: Structures hold different data types together, simplifying data management.
- **Custom Data Types**: Useful for representing complex data such as sensor data, where each field represents a specific characteristic.

Syntax

```
struct {
    type member;
} structName;
```

Syntax Explanation

- `struct`: Keyword for defining a structure.
- `type`: Data type of the structure members.
- `member`: Each data field within the structure.
- `structName`: The name of the structure variable.

Simple Code Example

```
struct SensorData {
    int id;
    float reading;
};
```

Code Example Explanation

- Defines a structure `SensorData` with an integer field `id` and a float field `reading`.

Notes

- Structures can be nested and used as arrays, allowing for highly flexible data management.

Warnings

- Take care with memory alignment; misaligned structures can cause access errors on certain architectures.

Relevant Project Section
Project Name
Sensor Data Logger with Multiple Data Types
Project Goal
Use different data types to record and manage data from a sensor on a RISC-V microcontroller, storing data such as sensor ID, reading value, and status.
RISC-V Development Environment
The project will use **PlatformIO** in **Visual Studio Code**. PlatformIO provides tools for building, uploading, and debugging code for RISC-V microcontrollers.
RISC-V Microcontroller
This example uses the **SiFive HiFive1 Rev B** microcontroller, based on the SiFive Freedom E310 RISC-V core, ideal for embedded applications.
Requirement Components
- **SIFIve HIFIve1 Rev B RISC-V Microcontroller**
- **Sensor** (e.g., temperature sensor) connected to an analog or digital input pin
- **LED** for indicating data logging activity

Component Connection Table

Component	RISC-V Pin	Additional Notes
Sensor	Analog Pin	Reads sensor data for logging
LED	GPIO Pin	Indicates activity during data logging

Connection Analysis
The sensor provides data that is logged by the microcontroller. The LED lights up to indicate logging is active, while the program stores multiple data types, including integer, float, and character.
Program Software Setup
1. Open **Visual Studio Code** with PlatformIO.
2. Create a new PlatformIO project for the **SiFive HiFive1 Rev B** board.
3. Define a structure to represent sensor data and variables for different data types.

Project Code

```c
#include <stdint.h>
#include "hifive1_gpio.h"  // Adjust for your SDK as needed
struct SensorData {
    int id;
    float reading;
    char status;
};
const int SENSOR_PIN = 0; // Example analog pin for sensor
const int LED_PIN = 13;   // Example GPIO pin for LED

void setup() {
    GPIO_DIR |= (1 << LED_PIN);      // Set LED_PIN as output
    GPIO_OUT &= ~(1 << LED_PIN);     // Initialize LED off
}
float readSensorData() {
    // Simulated sensor read function
    return 23.5;   // Placeholder value
}
void logSensorData(struct SensorData data) {
    // Simulated data logging function
    // Print or store the data as needed
}
int main() {
    setup();

    struct SensorData sensor;
    sensor.id = 1;
    sensor.status = 'A'; // 'A' for active

    while (1) {
        GPIO_OUT |= (1 << LED_PIN);           // Turn on LED to indicate
logging
        sensor.reading = readSensorData(); // Get sensor reading
        logSensorData(sensor);             // Log the sensor data
        GPIO_OUT &= ~(1 << LED_PIN);       // Turn off LED

        for (volatile int i = 0; i < 100000; i++); // Delay for next
read
    }
}
```

Save and Run

1. Save, compile, and upload the code to the **SiFive HiFive1 Rev B** board using PlatformIO.
2. Observe the LED indicating data logging, while the program logs and processes multiple data types.

Check Output

- The LED should blink to show data logging activity. The program reads, stores, and logs sensor data using different data types effectively.

Variable Scope and Variable Management in C for RISC-V Microcontrollers

Chapter Overview

In embedded programming with RISC-V microcontrollers, understanding variable scope and effective variable management is essential. Variable scope determines where a variable can be accessed within the code, and proper variable management ensures optimal memory usage and program stability. Local, global, and static variables each have distinct roles in embedded systems, and knowing when and where to use them is crucial for memory efficiency, debugging, and reducing power consumption.

Chapter Goal

- Understand different types of variable scope (local, global, and static) in C programming for RISC-V microcontrollers.
- Learn techniques for efficient variable management, including memory allocation and variable lifetime control.
- Implement a project that demonstrates practical applications of variable scope and management, optimizing memory usage.

Rules

- **Use Local Variables When Possible**: Limit variable scope to where it is needed to conserve memory.
- **Avoid Excessive Global Variables**: Only use global variables for data that needs to be accessed across multiple functions.
- **Leverage Static Variables for Consistent States**: Use static variables to retain values across function calls.
- **Minimize Memory Usage**: Declare variables in the smallest scope needed and release them when they are no longer required.

Brief Introduction to Variable Scope

Variable scope in C defines where a variable can be accessed in a program. Local variables exist only within specific functions, while global variables are accessible throughout the program. Static variables retain their values between function calls, which is useful in embedded programming for managing states. Understanding variable scope helps prevent memory overuse, avoids conflicts, and ensures the program runs efficiently, especially on memory-limited devices like RISC-V microcontrollers.

Syntax Table

Serial No	Topic	Syntax	Simple Example
1	Local Variable	`type varName;`	`int counter;`
2	Global Variable	`type varName;` (outside functions)	`int total;`
3	Static Variable	`static type varName;`	`static int count;`
4	Variable Initialization	`type varName = value;`	`int value = 5;`
5	Extern Keyword	`extern type varName;`	`extern int total;`

Detailed Breakdown for Each Command
1. Local Variable
What is Local Variable?

A local variable is declared within a function and is only accessible within that function. Local variables are created when the function is called and destroyed when it exits, making them ideal for temporary values.

Use Purpose

- **Temporary Data Storage**: Store values that are only needed within a specific function.
- **Avoid Memory Waste**: Local variables occupy memory only during function execution.

Syntax

```
type varName;
```

Syntax Explanation

- `type`: Specifies the data type of the variable, such as `int`, `float`, or `char`.
- `varName`: The name of the variable, which is only accessible within its declaring function.

Simple Code Example

```
void calculate() {
    int result = 0; // Local variable
}
```

Code Example Explanation

- Declares a local integer variable `result` inside the `calculate` function, which can only be accessed within this function.

Notes

- Local variables are automatically deallocated when the function finishes, freeing up memory.

Warnings

- Accessing a local variable outside its function will cause a compilation error.

2. Global Variable

What is Global Variable?
A global variable is declared outside any function, typically at the beginning of a program, and is accessible throughout the entire program. Global variables persist for the program's duration.

Use Purpose

- **Share Data Across Functions**: Useful for values that need to be accessed by multiple functions, such as configuration data.
- **Persistent Storage**: Retains its value throughout program execution.

Syntax

```
type varName;
```

Syntax Explanation

- **type**: Specifies the data type of the variable.
- **varName**: The variable name, accessible anywhere in the program.

Simple Code Example

```
int total; // Global variable
```

Code Example Explanation

- Declares total as a global variable, accessible by any function within the program.

Notes

- Global variables are initialized to zero by default.

Warnings

- Excessive use of global variables can lead to memory inefficiencies and debugging challenges.

3. Static Variable

What is Static Variable?
A static variable retains its value between function calls, allowing it to act as persistent storage within the function where it's declared.

Use Purpose

- **Maintain State Across Calls**: Ideal for counters or values that need to persist between function executions.
- **Limit Scope with Persistence**: Static variables are limited to the function they are declared in but retain their value.

Syntax

```
static type varName;
```

Syntax Explanation

- **static**: Modifier that keeps the variable's value even after the function exits.
- **type**: Specifies the data type.
- **varName**: The name of the variable, accessible only within its declaring function.

Simple Code Example

```
void track() {
    static int callCount = 0; // Static variable
    callCount++;
}
```

Code Example Explanation
- `callCount` is a static variable that increments each time `track` is called, retaining its value across calls.

Notes
- Static variables are initialized only once and keep their value between function calls.

Warnings
- Static variables are stored in global memory, so use them sparingly to avoid memory constraints.

4. Variable Initialization

What is Variable Initialization?
Initialization assigns an initial value to a variable when it is declared, ensuring it starts with a known value, especially important for local variables.

Use Purpose

- **Avoid Unpredictable Values**: Ensures variables start with a defined value.
- **Control Initial State**: Helps set counters, flags, and accumulators to a known starting point.

Syntax

```
type varName = value;
```

Syntax Explanation

- **type**: The data type of the variable.
- **varName**: The name of the variable.
- **value**: The initial value assigned to the variable.

Simple Code Example

```
int value = 5;
```

Code Example Explanation

- Declares an integer variable value with an initial value of 5.

Notes
- Always initialize variables that do not have default values (e.g., local variables).

Warnings

- Ensure the value type matches the variable type to avoid unexpected results.

5. Extern Keyword

What is Extern Keyword?

The `extern` keyword allows a variable to be used across multiple files. It declares a variable without defining it, assuming its definition exists elsewhere in the code.

Use Purpose

- **Share Global Variables Across Files**: Useful for large programs where variables need to be accessible across different modules.
- **Modularize Code**: Allows breaking code into multiple files without redefining variables.

Syntax

```
extern type varName;
```

Syntax Explanation

- **`extern`**: Indicates that the variable is defined in another file.
- **`type`**: Data type of the variable.
- **`varName`**: Name of the variable to be shared across files.

Simple Code Example

```
extern int total;
```

Code Example Explanation

- Declares that `total` is a variable defined in another file, allowing it to be accessed here.

Notes
- Place `extern` declarations in header files to share variables across multiple C files.

Warnings
- Ensure variables with `extern` are defined only once; multiple definitions cause errors.

Relevant Project Section

Project Name

Button-Controlled LED with Variable Scope Management

Project Goal

Create a program on the RISC-V microcontroller to toggle an LED using a button press, demonstrating the use of local, global, and static variables to manage state and functionality efficiently.

RISC-V Development Environment

This project will use **PlatformIO** in **Visual Studio Code** to build, upload, and debug the program on the RISC-V microcontroller.

RISC-V Microcontroller

This example uses the **SiFive HiFive1 Rev B** microcontroller, based on the SiFive Freedom E310 RISC-V core, suitable for embedded applications.

Requirement Components

- **SiFive HiFive1 Rev B RISC-V Microcontroller**
- **Button** connected to an input pin
- **LED** connected to an output pin

Component Connection Table

Component	RISC-V Pin	Additional Notes
Button	GPIO Pin	Used to control LED toggle function
LED	GPIO Pin	LED toggles on and off based on button

Connection Analysis

The button's state is read to determine whether the LED should toggle on or off. Global variables manage the button's state, static variables maintain the LED state between function calls, and local variables temporarily store values within the function.

Program Software Setup

1. Open **Visual Studio Code** with PlatformIO.
2. Create a new PlatformIO project and select **SiFive HiFive1 Rev B** as the board.
3. Implement code to toggle the LED based on button press, managing variable scope effectively.

Project Code

```c
#include <stdint.h>
#include "hifive1_gpio.h" // Adjust for your SDK

const int BUTTON_PIN = 2; // GPIO pin for button
const int LED_PIN = 13;   // GPIO pin for LED

// Global variable to store button state
int buttonState = 0;
void setup() {
    GPIO_DIR |= (1 << LED_PIN);        // Set LED_PIN as output
    GPIO_DIR &= ~(1 << BUTTON_PIN);    // Set BUTTON_PIN as input
    GPIO_OUT &= ~(1 << LED_PIN);       // Initialize LED off
}
void toggleLED() {
    static int ledState = 0; // Static variable to retain LED state

    if (ledState) {
        GPIO_OUT &= ~(1 << LED_PIN); // Turn off LED
    } else {
        GPIO_OUT |= (1 << LED_PIN);  // Turn on LED
    }
    ledState = !ledState; // Toggle ledState for next call
}
int main() {
    setup();

    while (1) {
        int currentButtonState = (GPIO_IN & (1 << BUTTON_PIN)) != 0; //
Local variable

        if (currentButtonState != buttonState) {
            if (currentButtonState == 1) { // Button pressed
                toggleLED(); // Toggle LED state
            }
            buttonState = currentButtonState; // Update global button
state
        }

        for (volatile int i = 0; i < 10000; i++); // Debounce delay
    }
}
```

Save and Run

1. Save, compile, and upload the code to the **SiFive HiFive1 Rev B** board using PlatformIO.
2. Press the button to toggle the LED state, verifying that variable scope is managed correctly.

Check Output

- The LED should toggle on or off each time the button is pressed. The program uses local, global, and static variables to handle the button state, LED state, and temporary values.

Digital I/O in C for RISC-V Microcontrollers

Chapter Overview

Digital I/O (Input/Output) operations enable a RISC-V microcontroller to interface with external devices like LEDs, buttons, and sensors. Digital pins can be configured as either inputs or outputs, allowing the microcontroller to read digital signals (HIGH/LOW) or control external devices. This chapter covers configuring and using digital I/O on RISC-V microcontrollers, including setting pin direction and reading/writing values to GPIO pins.

Chapter Goal

- Understand digital I/O operations on RISC-V microcontrollers.
- Learn how to set pins as inputs or outputs and read/write digital values.
- Implement a practical project to control an LED with a button.

Rules

- **Configure Pin Direction Correctly**: Always set a pin as INPUT or OUTPUT before using it.
- **Debounce Inputs**: Use software debouncing for buttons to prevent false triggers.
- **Check Voltage and Current Limits**: Ensure connected devices are within the microcontroller's I/O pin voltage/current ratings.
- **Use Pull-Up/Down Resistors for Inputs**: Improves reliability when reading button or switch states.

Brief Introduction to Digital I/O

RISC-V microcontrollers use digital I/O pins for input or output control. In INPUT mode, the microcontroller reads external signals as HIGH or LOW. In OUTPUT mode, it controls connected devices by setting pins HIGH or LOW. Configuring I/O pins effectively is crucial for reliable interaction with external components.

Syntax Table

Serial No	Topic	Syntax	Simple Example
1	Set Pin as Output	`` `GPIO_DIR ``	`= (1 << PIN);`
2	Set Pin as Input	`GPIO_DIR &= ~(1 << PIN);`	`GPIO_DIR &= ~(1 << 3);`
3	Write HIGH to Pin	`` `GPIO_OUT ``	`= (1 << PIN);`
4	Write LOW to Pin	`GPIO_OUT &= ~(1 << PIN);`	`GPIO_OUT &= ~(1 << 2);`
5	Read Pin State	`GPIO_IN & (1 << PIN)`	`GPIO_IN & (1 << 3)`

Detailed Breakdown for Each Command

1. Set Pin as Output

What is Setting a Pin as Output?
Configuring a pin as output allows the microcontroller to control the voltage level on that pin, enabling it to turn external devices like LEDs on or off.

Use Purpose

- **Control External Devices**: In output mode, the microcontroller can send HIGH or LOW signals to devices connected to the pin, such as LEDs or relays.
- **Enable Writing Digital States**: Required before setting a pin to HIGH or LOW to avoid undefined behavior.

Syntax

```
GPIO_DIR |= (1 << PIN);
```

Syntax Explanation

- **GPIO_DIR**: This register configures the direction of GPIO pins on the microcontroller. Each bit in this register corresponds to a specific pin; setting a bit to 1 makes the pin an OUTPUT, and setting it to 0 makes the pin an INPUT.
- **|=**: The bitwise OR-assignment operator modifies specific bits without affecting other bits. It is used here to set the bit for the desired pin while leaving other pins' configurations unchanged.
- **(1 << PIN)**: This expression shifts the bit "1" to the left by the number of positions specified by PIN. For example, if PIN is 2, (1 << PIN) produces 0b00000100, targeting pin 2 in the GPIO_DIR register and setting it as OUTPUT.

Simple Code Example

```
GPIO_DIR |= (1 << 2);
```

Code Example Explanation

- Sets pin 2 as an OUTPUT, allowing the microcontroller to control the connected device by sending a HIGH or LOW signal.

Notes

- Set a pin as OUTPUT before writing HIGH or LOW to avoid errors or damage to the microcontroller.

Warnings

- Ensure the component connected to the output pin does not exceed the pin's voltage and current ratings to avoid damage.

2. Set Pin as Input

What is Setting a Pin as Input?

Setting a pin as input configures it to read signals from external components like buttons or sensors. In this mode, the microcontroller can detect if the external signal is HIGH or LOW.

Use Purpose

- **Read External Signals**: Enables the microcontroller to sense the state of external devices such as buttons, switches, or digital sensors.
- **Prepare for Digital Read Operations**: Setting a pin as input is necessary before reading its state.

Syntax

```
GPIO_DIR &= ~(1 << PIN);
```

Syntax Explanation

- **GPIO_DIR**: Register to configure the direction of GPIO pins, where each bit corresponds to a pin on the microcontroller. Setting a bit to 0 makes the pin an INPUT.
- **&=**: The bitwise AND-assignment operator is used to clear the bit without affecting the other bits in GPIO_DIR. By using &=, only the specified pin is modified.
- **~(1 << PIN)**: This expression shifts 1 left by PIN positions, and the ~ (bitwise NOT) inverts the result. For example, if PIN is 3, (1 << PIN) gives 0b00001000, and ~(1 << PIN) becomes 0b11110111, clearing the 3rd bit.

Simple Code Example

```
GPIO_DIR &= ~(1 << 3);
```

Code Example Explanation

- Sets pin 3 as an INPUT, allowing it to receive and read signals from external devices, such as detecting a button press.

Notes

- When reading button states, consider using a pull-up or pull-down resistor to avoid unreliable or floating input values.

Warnings

- An input pin left unconnected or "floating" may pick up electrical noise, resulting in unpredictable readings.

---

3. Write HIGH to Pin

What is Writing HIGH to a Pin?
Writing HIGH to a pin that is set as OUTPUT makes it supply a voltage level, typically equivalent to the microcontroller's supply voltage (e.g., 3.3V or 5V). This can activate or turn on the connected device.

Use Purpose

- **Turn ON External Devices**: Sets connected devices, such as LEDs or relays, to an active state.
- **Signal HIGH in Digital Communication**: Used to represent a HIGH signal in digital applications.

Syntax
```
GPIO_OUT |= (1 << PIN);
```
Syntax Explanation
- **GPIO_OUT**: Register for controlling the output state of GPIO pins. Each bit corresponds to a specific pin; setting the bit to 1 makes the pin HIGH, and setting it to 0 makes it LOW.
- **|=**: The OR-assignment operator, which modifies only the bit for the specified pin, allowing other bits in GPIO_OUT to remain unchanged.
- **(1 << PIN)**: Shifts 1 to the left by the specified number of positions, aligning it with the bit for the desired pin. For example, (1 << 2) would set pin 2 in GPIO_OUT to HIGH.

Simple Code Example

```
GPIO_OUT |= (1 << 2);
```

Code Example Explanation

- Sets pin 2 to HIGH, applying a voltage to the pin and potentially turning on a connected device, such as an LED.

Notes

- Ensure that the pin is configured as OUTPUT before writing a HIGH signal to avoid potential issues.

Warnings

- If a connected device draws too much current, it may damage the pin. Check the current ratings for safe operation.

---

4. Write LOW to Pin

What is Writing LOW to a Pin?

Writing LOW to an output-configured pin pulls it to ground (0V), deactivating connected devices such as LEDs or relays.

Use Purpose

- **Turn OFF External Devices**: Pulling a pin to LOW turns off devices, like setting an LED to off.
- **Signal LOW in Digital Communication**: Represents a LOW or 0 signal in digital systems.

Syntax

```
GPIO_OUT &= ~(1 << PIN);
```

Syntax Explanation

- **GPIO_OUT**: The register controlling the output state of GPIO pins.
- **&=**: The AND-assignment operator, used to clear (set to 0) the bit associated with the pin.
- **~(1 << PIN)**: Shifts 1 to the left by the specified number of positions to match the pin, then inverts the result. For example, ~(1 << 2) results in 0b11111011, clearing the 2nd bit in GPIO_OUT and setting it LOW.

Simple Code Example

```
GPIO_OUT &= ~(1 << 2);
```

Code Example Explanation

- Sets pin 2 to LOW, deactivating any connected device, such as turning off an LED.

Notes

- To prevent unnecessary flickering or rapid switching, add delays between HIGH and LOW signals.

Warnings

- Avoid changing the output state of pins too quickly, as it may lead to undesired behaviors, such as power spikes.

---

5. Read Pin State
What is Reading Pin State?
Reading a pin's state allows the microcontroller to detect if an input-configured pin is HIGH or LOW, useful for button presses, switches, or sensor signals.
Use Purpose
- **Detect Button Presses**: Helps determine if a button or switch is activated.
- **Monitor External Signals**: Reads the status of devices like digital sensors.
Syntax

```
GPIO_IN & (1 << PIN)
```

Syntax Explanation
- **GPIO_IN**: Register for reading the current state of GPIO pins. Each bit represents the state of a corresponding pin.
- **&**: Bitwise AND operator, which isolates the specific bit associated with the pin, allowing for targeted state checking.
- **(1 << PIN)**: Shifts the bit 1 to the specified pin's position, creating a mask to isolate the state of that pin in GPIO_IN.

Simple Code Example

```
if (GPIO_IN & (1 << 3)) {
    // Pin 3 is HIGH
}
```

Code Example Explanation

- Checks if pin 3 is HIGH by isolating its state using $(1 << 3)$ in combination with `GPIO_IN`.

Notes

- Implement debouncing to ensure accurate button state reading.

Warnings

- Unconnected or floating input pins may give unreliable readings; connect them to a pull-up or pull-down resistor as needed.

Relevant Project Section

Project Name
Button-Controlled LED

Project Goal
Use digital I/O on a RISC-V microcontroller to toggle an LED when a button is pressed, demonstrating the basics of reading input and writing output.

RISC-V Development Environment
We will use **PlatformIO** with **Visual Studio Code** to build, upload, and debug the program.

RISC-V Microcontroller
This example uses the **SiFive HiFive1 Rev B** microcontroller, based on the SiFive Freedom E310 RISC-V core.

Requirement Components

- **SiFive HiFive1 Rev B Microcontroller**
- **Button** connected to an input pin
- **LED** connected to an output pin

Component Connection Table

Component	RISC-V Pin	Additional Notes
Button	GPIO Pin	Used to control LED toggle functionality
LED	GPIO Pin	Turns on/off based on button state

Connection Analysis

In this project, the button provides input to the microcontroller, allowing it to detect when the button is pressed. When a press is detected, the microcontroller toggles the state of an LED. The button is connected to a GPIO pin configured as an INPUT, while the LED is connected to a GPIO pin configured as an OUTPUT.

Program Software Setup

1. Open **Visual Studio Code** with **PlatformIO** installed.
2. Create a new PlatformIO project and select **SiFive HiFive1 Rev B** as the board.
3. Write code to initialize the LED and button pins, read the button's state, and toggle the LED accordingly.

Project Code

```
#include <stdint.h>
#include "hifive1_gpio.h"  // Include GPIO library (adjust for your
SDK)

const int BUTTON_PIN = 2; // Example GPIO pin for the button
const int LED_PIN = 13;   // Example GPIO pin for the LED

// Variable to keep track of the LED state
int ledState = 0;
```

```c
void setup() {
    // Set LED pin as OUTPUT
    GPIO_DIR |= (1 << LED_PIN);
    // Set BUTTON pin as INPUT
    GPIO_DIR &= ~(1 << BUTTON_PIN);
    // Initialize LED to be OFF
    GPIO_OUT &= ~(1 << LED_PIN);
}

void toggleLED() {
    if (ledState) {
        // Turn off LED if it's currently on
        GPIO_OUT &= ~(1 << LED_PIN);
    } else {
        // Turn on LED if it's currently off
        GPIO_OUT |= (1 << LED_PIN);
    }
    // Toggle the ledState variable to keep track
    ledState = !ledState;
}

int main() {
    setup();

    while (1) {
        // Read the current state of the button
        int buttonState = (GPIO_IN & (1 << BUTTON_PIN)) != 0;

        // If button is pressed, toggle LED
        if (buttonState) {
            toggleLED();
            // Debounce delay to prevent multiple toggles on a single
press
            for (volatile int i = 0; i < 100000; i++);  // Simple delay
        }

        // Small delay to avoid rapid re-checking
        for (volatile int i = 0; i < 1000; i++);
    }
}
```

Save and Run

1. Save, compile, and upload the code to the **SiFive HiFive1 Rev B** board using PlatformIO.
2. Press the button to toggle the LED's state, observing it turn on or off with each press.

Check Output

- The LED should toggle between ON and OFF with each press of the button. This behavior confirms that the microcontroller can successfully read the button's state and control the LED through digital I/O.

Analog I/O in C for RISC-V Microcontrollers

Chapter Overview

Analog I/O (Input/Output) operations allow a RISC-V microcontroller to interact with real-world analog signals. Unlike digital signals, which are binary (HIGH or LOW), analog signals vary continuously, allowing the microcontroller to interpret values like voltage levels, sensor readings, and other real-time data. Analog-to-Digital Conversion (ADC) is essential in embedded systems to read analog inputs, while Digital-to-Analog Conversion (DAC) outputs can simulate analog signals. This chapter covers configuring and using analog I/O on RISC-V microcontrollers and includes a practical project to measure a sensor's analog output.

Chapter Goal

- Understand the basics of Analog I/O, including ADC and DAC operations on RISC-V microcontrollers.
- Learn the syntax for configuring analog inputs, performing ADC, and interpreting values.
- Implement a project to read an analog sensor and display the interpreted result.

Rules

- **Set Up ADC Channels Correctly**: Configure the correct pin and channel before reading analog inputs.
- **Use Scaling Calculations**: For interpreting ADC values, use calculations to scale readings to meaningful units.
- **Consider Signal Filtering**: Analog signals may require filtering (hardware or software) for accurate readings.
- **Optimize Sampling Rate**: Adjust the sampling rate based on application requirements, balancing accuracy and speed.

Brief Introduction to Analog I/O
Analog signals vary over a range, unlike digital signals which are binary. In RISC-V microcontrollers, ADC (Analog-to-Digital Conversion) converts these analog signals into digital values the microcontroller can process. ADC values are often scaled based on the resolution (e.g., 10-bit ADC provides values from 0 to 1023). DAC is used in applications that require analog outputs. By understanding ADC and DAC, you can effectively read real-world signals and output analog-like signals.

Explanation of ADC Voltage Calculation
An ADC (Analog-to-Digital Converter) converts an analog input voltage into a digital value. To calculate the corresponding voltage for a given ADC digital value, we use this formula:

$$Voltage = \left(\frac{ADC\ Value}{Max\ ADC\ Value}\right) \times Reference\ Voltage$$

Let's break this formula into components to understand better:
What is an ADC?

- An ADC samples an analog signal (voltage) and converts it into a digital number.
- The range of values the ADC can output depends on its resolution, which is defined by the number of bits it uses.

Example ADC Resolution Calculation
For a 10-bit ADC
The resolution of an ADC is determined by the formula:
$$2^n = \{Number\ of\ Levels\}$$

Where:
- n=Number of bits of the ADC

For a 10-bit ADC, the resolution is $2^{10} = 1024$ levels (values from 0 to 1023).

This means the ADC has 1024 possible levels, ranging from 0 to 1023.

For a 12-bit ADC

For a **12-bit ADC**, the resolution is:

$$2^n = \{Number\ of\ Levels\}$$

For a 12-bit ADC, the resolution is 2^12 = 4096levels (values from 0 to 4096).

Understanding the Formula

(a) Normalized Value

The normalized value is calculated as:

$$\frac{ADC\ Value}{Max\ ADC\ Value}$$

This part gives the **proportion of the reference voltage** represented by the ADC value.

For example:
- If the ADC Value is 512 (halfway in a 10-bit range), this fraction would be

$$\frac{512}{1024} \approx 0.5$$

This means the ADC value represents 50% of the reference voltage.

Reference Voltage

- The reference voltage defines the **maximum voltage** the ADC can measure.
- If the reference voltage is 3.3V, the ADC will map:
  - 0to 0V
  - 1023 (or Max ADC Value) to 3.3

(c) Multiply by Reference Voltage

- Multiplying the normalized value by the reference voltage converts the proportion into the actual voltage.

Step-by-Step Example

Imagine a system with:

- A **10-bit ADC** (Max ADC Value = 102310231023)
- A **Reference Voltage** of 5.0V5.0V5.0V
- A raw ADC reading of **256**

Step 1: Normalize the ADC Value

$$\frac{ADC\ Value}{Max\ ADC\ Value} = \frac{256}{1024} \approx 0.25$$

Step 2: Multiply by the Reference Voltage

Voltage=0.25×5.0=1.25V

So, an ADC value of 256 corresponds to 1.25V.

Visualisation

- ADC Resolution: 10-bit
- Reference Voltage: 3.3V

ADC Value	Proportion (ADCValue/1023)	Voltage (V)
0	0/1023=0.0	0.0V
256	256/1023≈0.25	0.25×3.3=0.825V
512	512/1023≈0.5	0.5×3.3=1.65V
768	768/1023≈0.75	0.75×3.3=2.475V
1023	1023/1023=1.0	1.0×3.3=3.3V

Syntax Table

Seri al No	Topic	Syntax	Simple Example
1	Initialize ADC	`ADC_INIT();`	`ADC_INIT();`
2	Set ADC Channel	`ADC_SELECT_CHANNE L(channel);`	`ADC_SELECT_CHANNE L(1);`
3	Start ADC Conversio n	`ADC_START_CONVERS ION();`	`ADC_START_CONVERS ION();`
4	Read ADC Result	`ADC_READ();`	`int value = ADC_READ();`
5	Convert to Voltage	`voltage = (value / 1023.0) * ref;`	`float voltage = (value / 1023.0) * 3.3;`

Detailed Breakdown for Each Command

1. Initialize ADC
What is ADC Initialization?
Initializing the ADC prepares the microcontroller to perform analog-to-digital conversions by configuring necessary settings such as reference voltage, resolution, and any required internal components.
Use Purpose

- **Set Up ADC Hardware**: Ensures the ADC is ready for use with all necessary configurations.
- **Prepare for Accurate Readings**: Ensures stable and accurate conversions by setting reference voltages and resolution.

Syntax

```
ADC_INIT();
```

Syntax Explanation

- **ADC_INIT**: This function typically initializes the ADC peripheral with default or user-defined configurations. It might include setting the ADC clock, enabling the ADC module, and setting the reference voltage.

Simple Code Example

```
ADC_INIT();
```

Code Example Explanation

- This code initializes the ADC module, making it ready for analog-to-digital conversions.

Notes

- Always initialize the ADC before starting any conversion to avoid incorrect results.

Warnings

- Ensure the reference voltage and resolution match the sensor requirements for accurate readings.

---

2. Set ADC Channel
What is Setting ADC Channel?
Setting the ADC channel configures which analog input pin the ADC will read from. Microcontrollers often support multiple analog channels, each corresponding to a specific pin.
Use Purpose
- **Select Analog Pin for Reading**: Directs the ADC to read from the correct pin.
- **Switch Between Channels**: Allows multiple analog sensors to be read by selecting different channels.

Syntax

```
ADC_SELECT_CHANNEL(channel);
```

Syntax Explanation

- **ADC_SELECT_CHANNEL**: This function selects the specified channel for the ADC conversion. The argument, `channel`, corresponds to the analog pin number or channel number configured in the microcontroller.

Simple Code Example

```
ADC_SELECT_CHANNEL(1);
```

Code Example Explanation

- This code sets the ADC to read from channel 1, allowing the ADC to read the analog signal from the corresponding pin.

Notes

- Some microcontrollers may use a dedicated function or register for channel selection.

Warnings

- Switching channels during conversion may lead to incorrect results. Ensure the conversion is complete before changing channels.

---

3. Start ADC Conversion
What is Starting an ADC Conversion?
Starting an ADC conversion instructs the ADC to sample the analog input and convert it into a digital value. This process must be completed before reading the result.
Use Purpose
- **Begin Analog Reading**: Initiates the conversion process to read the analog value.
- **Capture Current Signal**: Samples the input at the current signal level.

Syntax

```
ADC_START_CONVERSION();
```

Syntax Explanation

- **ADC_START_CONVERSION**: This function begins the analog-to-digital conversion process. When called, the ADC starts sampling the selected analog channel and converting the voltage into a digital value.

Simple Code Example

```
ADC_START_CONVERSION();
```

Code Example Explanation

- This code starts the ADC conversion process, beginning the reading and conversion of the analog signal on the selected channel.

Notes

- Conversion time may vary based on the ADC's resolution and clock speed.

Warnings

- Starting a new conversion before the current one completes can lead to inaccurate data.

---

4. Read ADC Result
What is Reading ADC Result?

Reading the ADC result retrieves the converted digital value, which represents the sampled analog voltage level in digital form. The result can then be used for calculations or further processing.

Use Purpose

- **Access Conversion Data**: Allows retrieval of the converted digital value representing the analog input.
- **Use for Calculations**: The digital value can be converted to a voltage or other units as needed.

Syntax

```
int value = ADC_READ();
```

Syntax Explanation

- **ADC_READ**: This function returns the digital result from the most recent ADC conversion. The value represents the sampled analog voltage, scaled according to the ADC's resolution.

Simple Code Example

```
int value = ADC_READ();
```

Code Example Explanation

- This code reads the digital value from the ADC, storing it in the variable `value`.

Notes

- The returned value's range depends on the ADC's resolution (e.g., 0–1023 for a 10-bit ADC).

Warnings

- Ensure the ADC conversion has completed before reading the result to avoid reading incomplete data.

---

5. Convert to Voltage
What is Converting to Voltage?

After reading the ADC result, you may need to convert it to a voltage level for meaningful interpretation. Using a known reference voltage and the ADC's resolution, the digital value can be scaled back to a voltage.

Use Purpose

- **Translate Digital Value**: Converts the ADC result into a real-world voltage.
- **Sensor Data Interpretation**: Allows accurate understanding of sensor readings in volts or other meaningful units.

Syntax

```
float voltage = (value / 1023.0) * reference;
```

Syntax Explanation

- **value**: The digital result from the ADC.
- **1023.0**: The maximum value for a 10-bit ADC, used here as a scaling factor. For other resolutions, this number should be adjusted (e.g., 4095.0 for a 12-bit ADC).
- **reference**: The reference voltage of the ADC, typically 3.3V or 5V.

Simple Code Example

```
float voltage = (value / 1023.0) * 3.3;
```

Code Example Explanation

- This converts the raw ADC value to a voltage level, assuming a reference voltage of 3.3V and a 10-bit ADC.

Notes

- The reference voltage should match the actual reference used for the ADC to ensure accurate results.

Warnings

- Incorrect scaling can lead to inaccurate voltage readings. Always confirm the ADC resolution and reference voltage.

Relevant Project Section

Project Name
Temperature Sensor Reader

Project Goal
Use an ADC on a RISC-V microcontroller to read an analog temperature sensor and convert the reading to a temperature value in degrees Celsius.

RISC-V Development Environment
This project will be built using **PlatformIO** in **Visual Studio Code**.

RISC-V Microcontroller
The **SiFive HiFive1 Rev B** microcontroller, based on the SiFive Freedom E310 RISC-V core, is used in this project.

Requirement Components

- **SiFive HiFive1 Rev B Microcontroller**
- **Analog Temperature Sensor** (e.g., TMP36) connected to an analog input pin
- **Display or Serial Monitor** for displaying temperature readings

Component Connection Table

Component	RISC-V Pin	Additional Notes
Temperature Sensor	ADC Pin	Analog sensor output connected
Display/Serial Out	UART/Serial	Used to display temperature output

Connection Analysis
The temperature sensor's analog output is read by the ADC on the microcontroller. The microcontroller converts the reading to a temperature value, which is displayed through the serial monitor or display.

Program Software Setup

1. Open **Visual Studio Code** and create a new project in **PlatformIO**.
2. Set up the ADC to read the temperature sensor's output.
3. Write code to initialize the ADC, start the conversion, read the result, and convert it to a temperature value.

Project Code

```c
#include <stdint.h>
#include <stdio.h>
#include "hifive1_adc.h"   // Replace with actual ADC library

#define REF_VOLTAGE 3.3   // Reference voltage for ADC
#define TEMP_PIN 1        // ADC pin for the temperature sensor

void setupADC() {
    ADC_INIT();                      // Initialize the ADC module
    ADC_SELECT_CHANNEL(TEMP_PIN); // Select the temperature sensor
channel
}

float readTemperature() {
    ADC_START_CONVERSION();   // Start ADC conversion
    int adcValue = ADC_READ(); // Read the ADC value

    // Convert ADC value to voltage
    float voltage = (adcValue / 1023.0) * REF_VOLTAGE;

    // Convert voltage to temperature (assumes TMP36 sensor)
    float temperatureC = (voltage - 0.5) * 100;
    return temperatureC;
}

int main() {
    setupADC();
    while (1) {
        float temperature = readTemperature();
        printf("Temperature: %.2f °C\n", temperature);   // Display
temperature

        for (volatile int i = 0; i < 1000000; i++); // Simple delay
    }
}
```

Save and Run

1. Save, compile, and upload the code to the **SiFive HiFive1 Rev B** board.
2. Open the serial monitor to view the temperature output.

Check Output

- The temperature in degrees Celsius should display on the serial monitor, updating periodically.

Advanced I/O in C for RISC-V Microcontrollers

Chapter Overview
Advanced I/O operations expand the functionality of digital and analog I/O by enabling the use of timers, interrupts, and communication protocols (such as SPI, I2C, and UART) to manage peripherals and handle complex tasks. These advanced I/O functions are crucial for precise control, high-speed data transfer, and efficient handling of real-time events, making them essential for embedded applications on RISC-V microcontrollers.

Chapter Goal

- Understand the basic principles of advanced I/O operations, including timers, interrupts, and communication protocols.
- Learn the syntax for configuring and using advanced I/O functions in RISC-V microcontrollers.
- Implement a project using PWM (Pulse Width Modulation) to control an LED's brightness.

Rules

- **Use Timers for Accurate Timing**: Timers offer high precision for managing time-sensitive tasks.
- **Handle Interrupts Carefully**: Ensure that interrupt routines are efficient to prevent system slowdown.
- **Set Up Communication Protocols Correctly**: Use SPI, I2C, or UART according to device specifications and requirements.
- **Optimize for Speed and Efficiency**: Minimize delays in I/O operations to achieve real-time performance.

Brief Introduction to Advanced I/O
Advanced I/O functionalities include timers, PWM, interrupts, and communication protocols. Timers allow precise timing control, PWM enables variable control of devices like LEDs and motors, interrupts provide efficient event handling, and protocols like SPI, I2C, and UART facilitate communication with sensors and other peripherals. Advanced I/O allows the microcontroller to handle complex tasks, enhancing the range of possible applications.

Syntax Table

Serial No	Topic	Syntax	Simple Example
1	Initialize Timer	`TIMER_INIT(period);`	`TIMER_INIT(1000);`
2	Set PWM Duty Cycle	`PWM_SET_DUTY(channel, dutyCycle);`	`PWM_SET_DUTY(1, 50);`
3	Enable Interrupt	`ENABLE_INTERRUPT(channel);`	`ENABLE_INTERRUPT(1);`
4	Initialize UART	`UART_INIT(baudRate);`	`UART_INIT(9600);`
5	SPI Data Transfer	`SPI_TRANSFER(data);`	`SPI_TRANSFER(0xFF);`

Detailed Breakdown for Each Command

1. Initialize Timer

What is Timer Initialization?
Initializing a timer sets up the microcontroller's internal timer, allowing it to generate precise timing events. Timers are useful for managing intervals, creating delays, and generating PWM signals.

Use Purpose

- **Time-Based Control**: Manage regular intervals for tasks, such as blinking LEDs or generating PWM signals.
- **Precise Delays**: Use timers for delays without CPU occupation, unlike software-based loops.

Syntax

```
TIMER_INIT(period);
```

Syntax Explanation

- **TIMER_INIT**: This function initializes a timer, setting up parameters like the counting period.
- **period**: The desired timing interval or frequency for the timer. For example, period = 1000 could represent 1000 microseconds (1 ms) based on the timer's configuration.

Simple Code Example

```
TIMER_INIT(1000);
```

Code Example Explanation

- This initializes a timer with a period of 1000 microseconds, allowing it to generate events at 1 kHz.

Notes

- Timer intervals depend on the microcontroller's clock frequency and prescaler settings.

Warnings

- Incorrect timer setup can cause delays or inaccurate timing events.

---

2. Set PWM Duty Cycle

What is Setting PWM Duty Cycle?
The PWM duty cycle determines the proportion of time a signal stays HIGH within each cycle, controlling the power delivered to devices like LEDs or motors.

Use Purpose

- **Control Brightness or Speed**: Adjust the duty cycle to control LED brightness or motor speed.
- **Efficient Power Management**: PWM allows precise control of power to devices, improving efficiency.

Syntax

```
PWM_SET_DUTY(channel, dutyCycle);
```

Syntax Explanation

- **PWM_SET_DUTY**: This function sets the PWM duty cycle on a specific channel.
- **channel**: The PWM output channel. Microcontrollers often have multiple PWM-capable pins, each controlled independently.
- **dutyCycle**: The desired duty cycle as a percentage (0–100%). A duty cycle of 50% keeps the signal HIGH for half the period.

Simple Code Example

```
PWM_SET_DUTY(1, 50);
```

Code Example Explanation

- Sets the duty cycle of PWM channel 1 to 50%, resulting in an even on-off cycle.

Notes

- Higher duty cycles correspond to longer "on" times, increasing brightness or speed in connected devices.

Warnings

- Exceeding 100% or using negative values can lead to unexpected behavior or errors.

---

3. Enable Interrupt

What is Enabling an Interrupt?

Interrupts allow the microcontroller to handle events immediately, without polling. When an interrupt occurs, the microcontroller temporarily pauses its main tasks to execute the interrupt service routine (ISR).

Use Purpose

- **Efficient Event Handling**: Respond to events like button presses without polling.
- **Minimize CPU Load**: The main program can focus on other tasks, triggering only when an interrupt occurs.

Syntax

```
ENABLE_INTERRUPT(channel);
```

Syntax Explanation

- **ENABLE_INTERRUPT**: Enables the interrupt for a specific channel or event.
- **channel**: Represents the source of the interrupt (e.g., timer, external pin).

Simple Code Example

```
ENABLE_INTERRUPT(1);
```

Code Example Explanation

- Enables an interrupt on channel 1, allowing the microcontroller to respond when an event occurs on this channel.

Notes

- Ensure that the ISR (Interrupt Service Routine) is defined for the specific interrupt source.

Warnings

- Avoid lengthy ISRs, as they can interfere with the main program's timing and performance.

4. Initialize UART

What is UART Initialization?
UART (Universal Asynchronous Receiver-Transmitter) is a protocol for serial communication. Initializing UART configures the baud rate and other settings for serial data transmission.

Use Purpose

- **Data Communication**: UART enables communication between the microcontroller and other devices like computers or modules.
- **Debugging**: UART is commonly used for debugging through serial monitoring.

Syntax
```
UART_INIT(baudRate);
```

Syntax Explanation

- **UART_INIT**: This function initializes the UART module with the specified communication settings.
- **baudRate**: Sets the data transfer rate (e.g., 9600, 115200). Higher baud rates allow faster data transfer but may require more stable connections.

Simple Code Example
```
UART_INIT(9600);
```

Code Example Explanation

- Initializes UART with a baud rate of 9600, suitable for standard serial communication.

Notes

- Ensure the baud rate matches the device on the receiving end for reliable communication.

5. SPI Data Transfer

What is SPI Data Transfer?

SPI (Serial Peripheral Interface) is a communication protocol used for high-speed data exchange. SPI data transfer sends or receives data between the microcontroller and peripherals like sensors or memory modules.

Use Purpose

- **High-Speed Communication**: SPI supports fast data transfer between microcontrollers and peripherals.
- **Support for Multiple Devices**: SPI can handle multiple devices by using separate chip select (CS) pins.

Syntax

```
SPI_TRANSFER(data);
```

Syntax Explanation

- **SPI_TRANSFER**: This function sends data over the SPI bus and often reads data simultaneously from the connected device.
- **data**: The data byte or word to be sent to the SPI device.

Simple Code Example

```
SPI_TRANSFER(0xFF);
```

Code Example Explanation

- Transfers the byte 0xFF over the SPI bus, potentially controlling or reading from an external device.

Notes

- Configure SPI mode (clock polarity and phase) to match the requirements of the connected device.

Warnings

- Incorrect SPI configuration may lead to communication errors.

Relevant Project Section

Project Name
LED Brightness Control Using PWM

Project Goal
Use PWM on a RISC-V microcontroller to control the brightness of an LED by varying the duty cycle, demonstrating the use of advanced I/O functions.

RISC-V Development Environment
This project uses **PlatformIO** in **Visual Studio Code**.

RISC-V Microcontroller
We'll use the **SiFive HiFive1 Rev B** microcontroller, which includes PWM-capable GPIO pins.

Requirement Components

- **SiFive HiFive1 Rev B Microcontroller**
- **LED** connected to a PWM-capable pin
- **Potentiometer** (optional) to adjust the duty cycle dynamically

Component Connection Table

Component	RISC-V Pin	Additional Notes
LED	PWM Pin	LED brightness controlled via PWM
Potentiometer	Analog Pin	(Optional) Used to adjust PWM duty cycle

Connection Analysis
The LED is connected to a PWM-capable pin on the microcontroller, allowing brightness control by varying the PWM duty cycle.
Optionally, a potentiometer can be connected to an analog pin to adjust the duty cycle in real time.

Program Software Setup

1. Open **Visual Studio Code** and create a new PlatformIO project.
2. Initialize PWM for the LED pin and, optionally, set up ADC to read the potentiometer input.
3. Write code to adjust the PWM duty cycle and control the LED brightness.

Project Code

```
#include <stdint.h>
#include "hifive1_pwm.h"  // Include PWM library (adjust as per SDK)

const int LED_PIN = 1; // PWM channel for LED

void setupPWM() {
    TIMER_INIT(1000);                 // Initialize timer for 1 ms
period
    PWM_SET_DUTY(LED_PIN, 50);        // Set initial duty cycle to 50%
}

void adjustBrightness(int dutyCycle) {
    if (dutyCycle >= 0 && dutyCycle <= 100) {
        PWM_SET_DUTY(LED_PIN, dutyCycle); // Adjust LED brightness
    }
}

int main() {
    setupPWM();

    while (1) {
        for (int duty = 0; duty <= 100; duty += 10) {
            adjustBrightness(duty); // Increase brightness
            for (volatile int i = 0; i < 100000; i++); // Simple delay
        }
        for (int duty = 100; duty >= 0; duty -= 10) {
            adjustBrightness(duty); // Decrease brightness
            for (volatile int i = 0; i < 100000; i++); // Simple delay
        }
    }
}
```

Save and Run

1. Save, compile, and upload the code to the **SiFive HiFive1 Rev B** board using PlatformIO.
2. Observe the LED brightness gradually increasing and decreasing, controlled by the PWM duty cycle.

Check Output

- The LED should brighten and dim in a smooth cycle, demonstrating effective PWM control.

Control Structures in C for RISC-V Microcontrollers

Chapter Overview
Control structures are essential programming constructs that dictate the flow of a program, allowing specific actions to be performed under given conditions or repeatedly. In embedded programming for RISC-V microcontrollers, control structures like if, for, while, and switch statements enable decision-making and looped operations critical for responding to sensor data, controlling actuators, or managing timing. This chapter covers the primary control structures, with examples relevant to embedded applications.

Chapter Goal
- Understand the main control structures (if, for, while, and switch) used in C programming.
- Learn to use these control structures for decision-making and looping to manage microcontroller tasks.
- Implement a project that uses control structures to read sensor data and perform actions based on conditions.

Rules
- **Use Clear Conditions in Loops**: Ensure loops terminate appropriately to avoid infinite loops.
- **Minimize Nested Control Structures**: Reduces complexity and improves readability and debugging.
- **Select the Right Control Structure**: Choose based on the task (e.g., if for conditions, for for counted loops).
- **Avoid Heavy Processing in Loops**: In embedded systems, prioritize efficiency to maintain performance.

Brief Introduction to Control Structures
Control structures manage the program flow, allowing the microcontroller to make decisions or execute repetitive tasks. if statements are used for conditional checks, for and while loops are for repeated operations, and switch allows handling multiple cases based on a variable's value. These structures are critical for managing sensor inputs, controlling peripherals, and executing tasks based on specific conditions.

Syntax Table

Serial No	Topic	Syntax	Simple Example
1	If Statement	`if (condition) { }`	`if (sensorValue > 50) { }`
2	For Loop	`for (init; condition; incr)`	`for (int i = 0; i < 10; i++)`
3	While Loop	`while (condition) { }`	`while (sensorValue < 50) { }`
4	Do-While Loop	`do { } while (condition);`	`do { } while (count < 5);`
5	Switch Case	`switch (variable) { case: }`	`switch (sensorMode) { case 1:`

Detailed Breakdown for Each Command

1. If Statement

What is an If Statement?

An `if` statement allows the microcontroller to evaluate a condition and execute code only if the condition is true. This enables decision-making, where actions are performed based on sensor readings or other variables.

Use Purpose

- **Condition-Based Actions**: Executes specific code based on a condition, ideal for responding to sensor data or status checks.
- **Error Checking**: Used to validate data or parameters before proceeding.

Syntax

```
if (condition) {
    // Code to execute if condition is true
}
```

Syntax Explanation

- **if**: Keyword introducing the conditional statement.
- **condition**: The expression evaluated as true or false (e.g., sensorValue > threshold).
- **{ }**: Curly braces enclose the code executed if the condition is true.

Simple Code Example

```
if (sensorValue > 50) {
    GPIO_OUT |= (1 << LED_PIN); // Turn on LED
}
```

Code Example Explanation

- Checks if sensorValue exceeds 50; if true, turns on an LED.

Notes

- Add else for alternative actions if the condition is false.

Warnings

- Complex conditions can reduce readability; simplify where possible.

---

2. For Loop

What is a For Loop?

A for loop repeats a block of code a set number of times, making it ideal for tasks requiring counted iterations, such as initializing multiple outputs or sampling data.

Use Purpose

- **Counted Repetition**: Performs a task a specified number of times, such as iterating through an array.
- **Stepwise Processing**: Useful for operations that increment or decrement values over each loop cycle.

Syntax

```
for (initialization; condition; increment) {
    // Code to execute on each iteration
}
```

Syntax Explanation

- **initialization**: Sets the starting value, often for a loop counter (e.g., int i = 0).
- **condition**: Defines the loop's stopping criterion; when false, the loop ends.
- **increment**: Updates the counter after each loop iteration, such as i++.

Simple Code Example

```
for (int i = 0; i < 5; i++) {
    GPIO_OUT ^= (1 << LED_PIN); // Toggle LED
}
```

Code Example Explanation

- Loops 5 times, toggling an LED on and off each time.

Notes

- for loops are ideal when the number of iterations is known beforehand.

Warnings

- Avoid modifying loop counters inside the loop body, as this can cause unexpected behavior.

3. While Loop

What is a While Loop?

A while loop repeatedly executes code as long as a specified condition remains true. It's suitable for tasks where the number of iterations depends on real-time variables or events.

Use Purpose

- **Continuous Monitoring**: Ideal for polling a sensor or waiting for a specific condition.
- **Indefinite Repetition**: Loops until an external condition changes.

Syntax

```
while (condition) {
    // Code to execute while condition is true
}
```

Syntax Explanation

- **while**: Keyword for starting a loop that depends on a condition.
- **condition**: Expression evaluated before each loop iteration; if false, the loop ends.

Simple Code Example

```
while (buttonPressed) {
    GPIO_OUT ^= (1 << LED_PIN); // Toggle LED
}
```

Code Example Explanation

- Continues toggling the LED while buttonPressed is true.

Notes
- Ensure there is an exit condition to avoid infinite loops.
Warnings
- Infinite loops may cause the microcontroller to hang if not controlled carefully.

4. Do-While Loop

What is a Do-While Loop?
A do-while loop executes code at least once, regardless of the condition, and then repeats if the condition is true. This loop is beneficial when an action must occur at least once before condition checking.

Use Purpose

- **Mandatory Single Execution**: Runs code once and repeats only if conditions are met.
- **User Prompts or Polling**: Useful for actions that should happen at least once.

Syntax

```
do {
    // Code to execute
} while (condition);
```

Syntax Explanation

- **do**: Starts the loop body, which is executed at least once.
- **while**: Tests the condition after executing the code block, repeating if true.

Simple Code Example

```
do {
    GPIO_OUT ^= (1 << LED_PIN); // Toggle LED once
} while (buttonPressed);
```

Code Example Explanation

- Toggles the LED once, and if buttonPressed is true, continues toggling until false.

Notes

- Suitable when you need guaranteed single execution before checking conditions.

5. Switch Case
What is a Switch Case?
A `switch` statement allows execution of different blocks of code based on the value of a variable. It's a streamlined alternative to multiple `if-else` statements and is useful for mode selection.

Use Purpose
- **Mode Selection**: Executes different actions based on specific cases.
- **Efficient Alternative to Multiple If-Else**: Cleaner and easier to read when handling multiple values.

Syntax
```
switch (variable) {
    case value1:
        // Code for case value1
        break;
    case value2:
        // Code for case value2
        break;
    default:
        // Code if no cases match
}
```

Syntax Explanation
- **switch**: Evaluates the variable and directs control to the matching case.
- **case**: Defines specific values to compare against the variable.
- **break**: Exits the switch after executing the matching case's code.
- **default**: Runs if none of the cases match.

Simple Code Example
```
switch (sensorMode) {
    case 1:
        GPIO_OUT |= (1 << LED_PIN); // Turn on LED
        break;
    case 2:
        GPIO_OUT &= ~(1 << LED_PIN); // Turn off LED
        break;
    default:
        GPIO_OUT ^= (1 << LED_PIN); // Toggle LED
}
```

Code Example Explanation

- Controls the LED state based on `sensorMode`. For `sensorMode` 1, the LED turns on; for 2, it turns off, and in other cases, it toggles.

Notes

- `switch` is more efficient than multiple `if-else` statements for cases with many possible values.

Warnings

- Missing `break` statements can cause unintended fall-through, where multiple cases are executed.

Relevant Project Section

Project Name
Temperature-Based Fan Controller

Project Goal
Use control structures to monitor temperature readings and control a fan's speed or state based on the temperature range, demonstrating the practical application of `if`, `while`, and `switch` statements.

RISC-V Development Environment
This project will use **PlatformIO** in **Visual Studio Code**.

RISC-V Microcontroller
We'll use the **SiFive HiFive1 Rev B** microcontroller, compatible with external sensor inputs.

Requirement Components

- **SiFive HiFive1 Rev B Microcontroller**
- **Temperature Sensor** connected to an analog input pin
- **Fan** (or LED) connected to a GPIO pin, indicating the fan's operational state

Component Connection Table

Component	RISC-V Pin	Additional Notes
Temperature Sensor	Analog Pin	Analog signal representing temperature
Fan/LED	GPIO Pin	Simulates fan operation based on temperature

Connection Analysis

The temperature sensor provides input to the microcontroller. Depending on the temperature, the microcontroller activates the fan (or toggles an LED) to indicate fan operation based on specified temperature ranges.

Program Software Setup

1. Open **Visual Studio Code** and set up a PlatformIO project.
2. Write code to read temperature values and implement control structures for fan control based on temperature ranges.

Project Code

```
#include <stdint.h>
#include <stdio.h>
#include "hifive1_adc.h"  // Replace with actual ADC library

#define TEMP_THRESHOLD_HIGH 30   // High temperature threshold
#define TEMP_THRESHOLD_LOW 20    // Low temperature threshold
#define FAN_PIN 13               // GPIO pin for fan/LED

void setup() {
    GPIO_DIR |= (1 << FAN_PIN); // Set FAN_PIN as output
    ADC_INIT();                 // Initialize ADC
    ADC_SELECT_CHANNEL(1);      // Select temperature sensor channel
}

int readTemperature() {
    ADC_START_CONVERSION();     // Start ADC conversion
    int adcValue = ADC_READ();  // Read ADC value
    float voltage = (adcValue / 1023.0) * 3.3;  // Convert to voltage
    int temperatureC = (voltage - 0.5) * 100;   // Convert voltage to
temperature
    return temperatureC;
}

int main() {
    setup();
```

```
    while (1) {
        int temp = readTemperature();

        if (temp > TEMP_THRESHOLD_HIGH) {
            GPIO_OUT |= (1 << FAN_PIN); // Turn on fan/LED if
temperature is high
        } else if (temp < TEMP_THRESHOLD_LOW) {
            GPIO_OUT &= ~(1 << FAN_PIN); // Turn off fan/LED if
temperature is low
        }

        printf("Temperature: %d C\n", temp); // Display temperature

        for (volatile int i = 0; i < 1000000; i++); // Simple delay
    }
}
```

Save and Run

1. Save, compile, and upload the code to the **SiFive HiFive1 Rev B** board.
2. Monitor the LED or fan state based on temperature readings.

Check Output

- The fan or LED should turn on or off based on the defined temperature thresholds, demonstrating effective use of if-else control structure.

Arithmetic Operators in C for RISC-V Microcontrollers

Chapter Overview
Arithmetic operators are fundamental tools in programming that perform mathematical operations such as addition, subtraction, multiplication, and division. In embedded programming for RISC-V microcontrollers, arithmetic operations are essential for processing sensor data, performing calculations, controlling devices, and managing system states. This chapter will cover the primary arithmetic operators used in C programming, their syntax, and applications in embedded systems.

Chapter Goal

- Understand the main arithmetic operators used in C (+, -, *, /, %) and how they function in RISC-V embedded programming.
- Learn how to use these operators for calculations, data processing, and control logic.
- Implement a project that utilizes arithmetic operations to process sensor data and control an output based on the result.

Rules

- **Use Appropriate Data Types**: Ensure data types match the operation to avoid overflow or precision errors.
- **Be Cautious with Division and Modulus**: Division by zero causes errors, and modulus is only applicable for integer data types.
- **Optimize Arithmetic Calculations**: Avoid unnecessary operations in loops or time-critical sections to improve efficiency.
- **Consider Integer Overflow**: In embedded systems with limited memory, take care to prevent overflow when performing arithmetic.

Brief Introduction to Arithmetic Operators
Arithmetic operators perform basic mathematical functions on
variables and values, allowing the manipulation of data in embedded
applications. With these operators, microcontrollers can perform
tasks like summing values, scaling sensor readings, calculating
percentages, and more. The primary arithmetic operators in C
include + (addition), - (subtraction), * (multiplication), / (division),
and % (modulus).

Syntax Table

Serial No	Topic	Syntax	Simple Example
1	Addition	a + b	int sum = a + b;
2	Subtraction	a - b	int diff = a - b;
3	Multiplication	a * b	int prod = a * b;
4	Division	a / b	int quotient = a / b;
5	Modulus	a % b	int remainder = a % b;

Detailed Breakdown for Each Command

1. Addition Operator (+)

What is Addition?
The addition operator + combines two values or variables, resulting
in their sum. It is widely used in embedded programming for
accumulating data, calculating totals, and summing values from
sensors.

Use Purpose

- **Data Accumulation**: Useful for summing sensor readings or incremental values.
- **Offset Calculation**: Adds an offset to a base value for calibration or positioning.

Syntax

```
a + b;
```

Syntax Explanation

- **a** and **b**: These are variables or values to be added. The result is the sum of a and b.

Simple Code Example

```
int a = 5;
int b = 10;
int sum = a + b;
```

Code Example Explanation

- Adds the values of a and b, storing the result in sum, which would equal 15.

Notes

- The addition operator is associative, so a + b + c is evaluated left to right.

Warnings

- Be mindful of overflow with large values, especially on smaller data types like uint8_t.

---

2. Subtraction Operator (-)
What is Subtraction?

The subtraction operator - calculates the difference between two values. It is useful in embedded systems for determining differences, such as error correction, and adjusting control variables.

Use Purpose

- **Difference Calculation**: Determines the difference between two readings.
- **Error Correction**: Used in control systems to calculate error values by subtracting actual values from target values.

Syntax

```
a - b;
```

Syntax Explanation

- **a** and **b**: Variables or values to be subtracted. The result is the difference between a and b.

Simple Code Example

```
int a = 15;
int b = 5;
int diff = a - b;
```

Code Example Explanation

- Subtracts b from a, storing the result in `diff`, which would equal 10.

Notes

- Subtraction is non-commutative; a - b is not the same as b - a.

Warnings

- Ensure values are within range to prevent underflow, especially with unsigned integers.

---

3. Multiplication Operator (*)
What is Multiplication?

The multiplication operator * calculates the product of two values. In embedded applications, it is commonly used for scaling values, calculating areas or distances, and managing sensor data.

Use Purpose

- **Scaling and Amplification**: Multiply sensor values by constants to scale readings.
- **Geometric Calculations**: Useful in applications involving areas, volumes, and distances.

Syntax

```
a * b;
```

Syntax Explanation

- **a** and **b**: Variables or values to be multiplied. The result is the product of a and b.

Simple Code Example

```
int a = 4;
int b = 5;
int prod = a * b;
```

Code Example Explanation

- Multiplies a and b, storing the result in prod, which would equal 20.

Notes

- Multiplication may quickly exceed smaller data types; consider using larger types like int32_t when needed.

Warnings

- Watch for overflow in calculations, especially when multiplying large values.

---

4. Division Operator (/)
What is Division?

The division operator / divides one value by another, producing a quotient. It's commonly used in embedded systems for averaging, scaling, and normalization.

Use Purpose

- **Averaging**: Sum values and divide by the number of readings to get an average.
- **Scaling Down**: Reduce sensor data or signals by a factor.

Syntax

```
a / b;
```

Syntax Explanation

- **a** and **b**: The dividend (a) and divisor (b). The result is the quotient of a divided by b.

Simple Code Example

```
int a = 20;
int b = 4;
int quotient = a / b;
```

Code Example Explanation

- Divides a by b, storing the result in `quotient`, which would equal 5.

Notes

- Division by zero is undefined and causes errors; always check that the divisor is not zero.

Warnings

- Integer division truncates results; use floating-point data types if fractional values are needed.

---

5. Modulus Operator (%)
What is Modulus?

The modulus operator % returns the remainder of a division. It is used primarily for operations involving cycles, patterns, or conditions.

Use Purpose

- **Cycle Management**: Use modulus to loop within a range (e.g., keeping values within a specific boundary).
- **Conditional Checks**: Check for divisibility (e.g., if a number is even or odd).

Syntax

```
a % b;
```

Syntax Explanation

- **a** and **b**: The dividend and divisor. The result is the remainder of a divided by b.

Simple Code Example

```
int a = 10;
int b = 3;
int remainder = a % b;
```

Code Example Explanation

- Divides a by b, with `remainder` storing the result of a % b, which would equal 1.

Notes

- Modulus is typically used with integer types.

Warnings

- Avoid using modulus with a divisor of zero, as it causes errors.

Relevant Project Section

Project Name
Distance Calculator Using Arithmetic Operations

Project Goal

Use arithmetic operators on a RISC-V microcontroller to calculate distance using sensor data. The project involves reading data from a hypothetical distance sensor and performing basic arithmetic to calculate an average distance and error from a target value.

RISC-V Development Environment

This project will be developed in **PlatformIO** using **Visual Studio Code**.

RISC-V Microcontroller

The **SiFive HiFive1 Rev B** microcontroller is used for this project.

Requirement Components

- **SiFive HiFive1 Rev B Microcontroller**
- **Distance Sensor** connected to an analog input pin
- **Display or Serial Output** for displaying results

Component Connection Table

Component	RISC-V Pin	Additional Notes
Distance Sensor	ADC Pin	Provides analog input for distance measurement
Display/Serial Out	UART/Serial	Displays calculated distance

Connection Analysis

The distance sensor's analog signal is converted to digital using the ADC. Arithmetic operations calculate the average distance over multiple readings and compare it to a target distance, displaying the result via the serial monitor.

Program Software Setup

1. Open **Visual Studio Code** and set up a new PlatformIO project.
2. Configure ADC to read distance sensor data.
3. Implement code to perform arithmetic calculations to determine average distance and check deviation from a target distance.

Project Code

```c
#include <stdint.h>
#include <stdio.h>
#include "hifive1_adc.h"  // Include ADC library

#define TARGET_DISTANCE 50  // Target distance in arbitrary units
#define READINGS 5          // Number of readings for averaging

void setup() {
    ADC_INIT();                 // Initialize ADC
    ADC_SELECT_CHANNEL(1);      // Select ADC channel for sensor
}

int readDistance() {
    ADC_START_CONVERSION();     // Start ADC conversion
    int adcValue = ADC_READ();  // Read ADC value
    return adcValue;            // Return raw sensor value
}

int calculateAverageDistance() {
    int sum = 0;
    for (int i = 0; i < READINGS; i++) {
        sum += readDistance(); // Accumulate sensor readings
    }
    int average = sum / READINGS; // Calculate average
    return average;
}

void displayDistance(int distance) {
    int error = TARGET_DISTANCE - distance; // Calculate error
    printf("Average Distance: %d\n", distance);
    printf("Error from Target: %d\n", error);
}
int main() {
    setup();

    while (1) {
        int averageDistance = calculateAverageDistance();
        displayDistance(averageDistance);

        for (volatile int i = 0; i < 1000000; i++); // Simple delay
    }
}
```

Save and Run

1. Save, compile, and upload the code to the **SiFive HiFive1 Rev B** board using PlatformIO.
2. Observe the average distance and error from the target displayed in the serial monitor.

Check Output

- The serial monitor should display the calculated average distance and the error from the target, updating periodically.

Comparison Operators in C for RISC-V Microcontrollers

Chapter Overview

Comparison operators allow programs to evaluate relationships between values, enabling decision-making based on conditions. In embedded programming for RISC-V microcontrollers, comparison operators help assess sensor data, control devices, and manage flow based on criteria. This chapter covers the primary comparison operators, their syntax, and applications in embedded systems.

Chapter Goal

- Understand how to use comparison operators (==, !=, >, <, >=, <=) in embedded C programming.
- Learn to apply these operators in decision-making processes to manage tasks and responses based on conditions.
- Implement a project that uses comparison operators to evaluate sensor data and control an output based on conditions.

Rules

- **Use Meaningful Conditions**: Keep conditions clear and logical for code readability and maintainability.
- **Avoid Complex Expressions**: Break down complex conditions into simpler expressions for efficiency.
- **Check for Data Type Compatibility**: Ensure that data types are compatible with comparison operations to avoid unexpected results.
- **Use Parentheses for Clarity**: Enclose complex expressions in parentheses to clarify evaluation order.

Brief Introduction to Comparison Operators

Comparison operators assess the relationship between two values, resulting in a boolean outcome (true or false). In C programming, these operators include == (equal), != (not equal), > (greater than), < (less than), >= (greater than or equal), and <= (less than or equal). Comparison operations are crucial for creating conditional statements that guide microcontroller behavior based on sensor data, user input, or state changes.

Syntax Table

Serial No	Topic	Syntax	Simple Example
1	Equal to	a == b	if (temp == 25)
2	Not Equal to	a != b	if (mode != 1)
3	Greater than	a > b	if (speed > 50)
4	Less than	a < b	if (voltage < 3.3)
5	Greater than or Equal	a >= b	if (score >= 100)
6	Less than or Equal	a <= b	if (distance <= 10)

Detailed Breakdown for Each Command

1. Equal to (==)

What is Equal to?

The == operator checks if two values are equal, returning true if they match. This operator is commonly used to verify conditions, such as checking if a sensor value equals a specified threshold.

Use Purpose

- **Equality Check**: Verify if two values are the same, such as verifying modes or states.
- **Conditional Execution**: Use in if statements to perform actions when two values match.

Syntax

```
a == b;
```

Syntax Explanation

- **a and b**: The two values or variables being compared. If a and b are equal, the result is `true`.

Simple Code Example

```
int temp = 25;
if (temp == 25) {
    GPIO_OUT |= (1 << FAN_PIN); // Turn on fan if temperature is 25
}
```

Code Example Explanation

- Checks if `temp` equals 25. If true, it turns on the fan.

Notes

- Use == for equality comparison; do not confuse it with = (assignment operator).

Warnings

- Ensure both values are of compatible data types to avoid unexpected behavior.

---

2. Not Equal to (!=)
What is Not Equal to?

The `!=` operator checks if two values are different, returning `true` if they do not match. It is useful for executing code when a value deviates from an expected state.

Use Purpose

- **Inequality Check**: Triggers actions if two values are not the same, such as handling error states.
- **Condition for Loops**: Use in loops to continue operations until values match.

Syntax

```
a != b;
```

Syntax Explanation

- **a and b**: The two values or variables being compared. The result is true if a and b are not equal.

Simple Code Example

```
int mode = 2;
if (mode != 1) {
    GPIO_OUT &= ~(1 << LED_PIN); // Turn off LED if mode is not 1
}
```

Code Example Explanation

- Checks if mode is not equal to 1. If true, it turns off the LED.

Notes

- != is particularly useful in cases where an exact match is not needed.

---

3. Greater than (>)
What is Greater than?
The > operator checks if one value is larger than another, commonly used in control systems to trigger actions when a value exceeds a limit.
Use Purpose
- **Threshold Checking**: Monitor if values exceed specific limits, like speed or temperature.
- **Event Triggers**: Execute code when a parameter surpasses a predefined value.
Syntax

```
a > b;
```

Syntax Explanation

- **a and b**: Values or variables being compared. The result is true if a is greater than b.

Simple Code Example

```
int speed = 60;
if (speed > 50) {
    GPIO_OUT |= (1 << ALARM_PIN); // Trigger alarm if speed is above 50
}
```

Code Example Explanation

- Checks if speed is greater than 50. If true, it triggers an alarm.

Notes

- Ideal for control limits and thresholds in embedded systems.

Warnings

- Ensure that values are within range to avoid incorrect comparisons.

---

4. Less than (<)

What is Less than?
The < operator checks if one value is smaller than another, useful for maintaining values within safe limits or managing low thresholds.

Use Purpose

- **Low-Level Checking**: Triggers actions if a value falls below a minimum threshold.
- **Control System Limits**: Ensures values remain within safe operating ranges.

Syntax

```
a < b;
```

Syntax Explanation

- **a and b**: Values or variables being compared. The result is true if a is less than b.

Simple Code Example

```
float voltage = 3.0;
if (voltage < 3.3) {
    GPIO_OUT |= (1 << LOW_POWER_PIN); // Activate low power mode if
voltage is below 3.3V
}
```

Code Example Explanation

- Checks if `voltage` is less than 3.3V. If true, it activates low power mode.

Notes

- Useful in applications with minimum operating thresholds.

Warnings

- Always ensure reliable sensor readings to avoid false triggers.

---

5. Greater than or Equal to (>=)

What is Greater than or Equal to?

The >= operator checks if one value is greater than or equal to another. This operator is helpful for ensuring values meet or exceed minimum criteria.

Use Purpose

- **Boundary Conditions**: Ensures that values meet or exceed a minimum level.
- **Control Logic**: Triggers events when a parameter reaches or surpasses a set point.

Syntax

```
a >= b;
```

Syntax Explanation

- **a and b**: Values or variables being compared. The result is true if a is greater than or equal to b.

Simple Code Example

```
int score = 100;
if (score >= 100) {
    GPIO_OUT |= (1 << SUCCESS_PIN); // Indicate success if score is 100
or more
}
```

Code Example Explanation

- Checks if `score` is greater than or equal to 100. If true, it indicates success.

Notes

- Ideal for handling minimum achievement criteria.

Warnings

- Ensure values are correctly initialized before comparison.

---

6. Less than or Equal to (<=)

What is Less than or Equal to?
The <= operator checks if one value is less than or equal to another. This operator is used for maximum limit checks, ensuring values stay below or at a set maximum.

Use Purpose

- **Upper Bound Control**: Prevents values from exceeding a maximum allowed level.
- **Safety Constraints**: Ensures that a parameter remains within acceptable limits.

Syntax

```
a <= b;
```

Syntax Explanation

- **a and b**: Values or variables being compared. The result is `true` if a is less than or equal to b.

Simple Code Example

```
int distance = 10;
if (distance <= 10) {
    GPIO_OUT &= ~(1 << STOP_PIN); // Stop motor if distance is 10 or
less
}
```

Code Example Explanation

- Checks if distance is less than or equal to 10. If true, it stops the motor.

Notes

- Helpful in applications with upper safety constraints.

Warnings

- Avoid using floating-point values in strict comparisons due to precision issues.

Relevant Project Section

Project Name
Temperature-Controlled Fan System

Project Goal
Use comparison operators on a RISC-V microcontroller to monitor temperature readings and control a fan based on different thresholds. This project demonstrates the use of comparison operators to manage device states based on sensor input.

RISC-V Development Environment
This project will use **PlatformIO** in **Visual Studio Code**.

RISC-V Microcontroller
We will use the **SiFive HiFive1 Rev B** microcontroller for this project.

Requirement Components

- **SiFive HiFive1 Rev B Microcontroller**
- **Temperature Sensor** connected to an analog input pin
- **Fan or LED** connected to a GPIO pin, simulating fan control based on temperature

Component Connection Table

Component	RISC-V Pin	Additional Notes
Temperature Sensor	ADC Pin	Analog signal representing temperature
Fan/LED	GPIO Pin	Turns on or off based on temperature

Connection Analysis

The temperature sensor provides analog input to the microcontroller, which converts it to a digital value. The microcontroller then uses comparison operators to evaluate the temperature and control the fan or LED according to predefined thresholds.

Program Software Setup

1. Open **Visual Studio Code** and create a new PlatformIO project.
2. Configure the ADC to read temperature data from the sensor.
3. Write code using comparison operators to control the fan or LED based on temperature thresholds.

Project Code

```
#include <stdint.h>
#include <stdio.h>
#include "hifive1_adc.h"  // Include ADC library

#define TEMP_HIGH_THRESHOLD 30   // High temperature threshold in
Celsius
#define TEMP_LOW_THRESHOLD 20    // Low temperature threshold in Celsius
#define FAN_PIN 13               // GPIO pin for fan/LED
```

```c
void setup() {
    GPIO_DIR |= (1 << FAN_PIN); // Set FAN_PIN as output
    ADC_INIT();                 // Initialize ADC
    ADC_SELECT_CHANNEL(1);      // Select ADC channel for temperature
sensor
}

int readTemperature() {
    ADC_START_CONVERSION();     // Start ADC conversion
    int adcValue = ADC_READ();  // Read ADC value
    float voltage = (adcValue / 1023.0) * 3.3;  // Convert to voltage
    int temperatureC = (voltage - 0.5) * 100;   // Convert voltage to
temperature
    return temperatureC;
}

int main() {
    setup();

    while (1) {
        int temp = readTemperature();

        if (temp >= TEMP_HIGH_THRESHOLD) {
            GPIO_OUT |= (1 << FAN_PIN); // Turn on fan if temperature
is high
        } else if (temp <= TEMP_LOW_THRESHOLD) {
            GPIO_OUT &= ~(1 << FAN_PIN); // Turn off fan if temperature
is low
        }

        printf("Temperature: %d C\n", temp); // Display temperature

        for (volatile int i = 0; i < 1000000; i++); // Simple delay
    }
}
```

Save and Run

1. Save, compile, and upload the code to the **SiFive HiFive1 Rev B** board using PlatformIO.
2. Monitor the LED or fan state based on the current temperature.

Check Output

- The fan or LED should turn on if the temperature exceeds the high threshold and turn off if it falls below the low threshold, demonstrating effective use of comparison operators.

Boolean Operators in C for RISC-V Microcontrollers

Chapter Overview

Boolean operators are essential in programming as they allow conditions to be combined, evaluated, and controlled. These operators (&&, | |, !) enable logical decision-making by combining multiple conditions, allowing embedded systems to respond to more complex scenarios. In RISC-V microcontroller programming, Boolean operators are used to create robust control logic for sensors, actuators, and various input/output combinations.

Chapter Goal

- Understand the primary Boolean operators (&&, | |, !) and their application in embedded C programming.
- Learn to use these operators to handle multiple conditions, improving control and decision-making.
- Implement a project to control an LED based on two sensor inputs, demonstrating the use of Boolean operators in practical applications.

Rules

- **Use Boolean Operators with Clarity**: Ensure that conditions are easy to read and understand, especially when using multiple operators.
- **Optimize Conditions**: Avoid redundant conditions to keep code efficient.
- **Handle Boolean Expressions Carefully**: Remember operator precedence when combining multiple conditions.
- **Minimize Nested Conditions**: Keep nesting minimal to improve readability and maintainability.

Brief Introduction to Boolean Operators

Boolean operators enable logical operations that result in a true or false outcome, helping microcontrollers make complex decisions. Common Boolean operators include && (AND), | | (OR), and ! (NOT). They allow combining conditions, such as checking if two or more sensor values meet criteria before performing an action. Boolean logic is a core part of embedded system programming, ensuring that microcontrollers respond accurately to multiple simultaneous conditions.

Syntax Table

Serial No	Topic	Syntax	Simple Example
1	Logical AND	a && b	if (sensor1 && sensor2)
3	Logical NOT	!a	if (!error)

Detailed Breakdown for Each Command

1. Logical AND (&&)

What is Logical AND?

The && operator checks if both conditions are true. It returns true only if both operands are true, making it ideal for situations where multiple conditions must be met.

Use Purpose

- **Multiple Condition Verification**: Ensures that all specified conditions are met before proceeding.
- **Safe Operations**: Useful for checking preconditions, such as ensuring multiple sensors are in a safe state.

Syntax

```
a && b;
```

Syntax Explanation

- **a and b**: These are the conditions being evaluated. The result is true only if both a and b are true.

Simple Code Example

```
int sensor1 = 1;
int sensor2 = 1;
if (sensor1 && sensor2) {
    GPIO_OUT |= (1 << LED_PIN); // Turn on LED if both sensors are
active
}
```

Code Example Explanation

- Checks if `sensor1` and `sensor2` are both true. If so, it turns on the LED.

Notes

- && short-circuits, meaning if the first condition is false, the second is not evaluated.

Warnings

- Ensure conditions are independent where necessary to avoid unexpected results from short-circuiting.

---

2. Logical OR (||)
What is Logical OR?

The || operator checks if at least one of the conditions is true. It returns true if either condition is true, making it useful when only one condition must be satisfied.

Use Purpose

- **Alternate Condition Checking**: Activates an operation if any one of multiple conditions is true.
- **Flexible Control**: Allows either of two or more states to satisfy a requirement.

Syntax

```
a || b;
```

Syntax Explanation

- **a and b**: These are the conditions being evaluated. The result is true if either a or b is true.

Simple Code Example

```
int mode = 2;
if (mode == 1 || mode == 2) {
    GPIO_OUT |= (1 << MOTOR_PIN); // Activate motor if mode is 1 or 2
}
```

Code Example Explanation

- Checks if mode is either 1 or 2. If true, it activates the motor.

Notes

- || also short-circuits, so if the first condition is true, the second is not evaluated.

Warnings

- Be cautious with short-circuiting if the second condition is necessary for the operation.

---

3. Logical NOT (!)

What is Logical NOT?
The ! operator inverts the result of a condition, turning true to false and vice versa. It is useful for toggling between states or checking for false conditions.

Use Purpose

- **Negate Conditions**: Inverts a condition's value, allowing code to check for a condition being false.
- **Error and Status Checking**: Commonly used to ensure a flag or error is not active.

Syntax
```
!a;
```
Syntax Explanation
- **a**: The condition being inverted. If a is true, !a returns false, and vice versa.

Simple Code Example
```
int error = 0;
if (!error) {
    GPIO_OUT |= (1 << LED_PIN); // Turn on LED if there is no error
}
```

Code Example Explanation

- Checks if `error` is false. If true, it turns on the LED.

Notes

- Use `!` carefully, as double negatives can make conditions harder to read.

Warnings

- Avoid excessive negation, as it can make logic difficult to understand.

Relevant Project Section

Project Name
Dual-Sensor Controlled LED System

Project Goal
Use Boolean operators on a RISC-V microcontroller to control an LED based on inputs from two sensors. The LED turns on if both sensors detect an object (AND condition) or if either sensor detects an object (OR condition), demonstrating the use of Boolean logic in control applications.

RISC-V Development Environment
This project will use **PlatformIO** in **Visual Studio Code**.

RISC-V Microcontroller
We will use the **SiFive HiFive1 Rev B** microcontroller for this project.

Requirement Components

- **SiFive HiFive1 Rev B Microcontroller**
- **Two Proximity Sensors** connected to GPIO pins as digital inputs
- **LED** connected to a GPIO pin as a digital output

Component Connection Table

Component	RISC-V Pin	Additional Notes
Proximity Sensor 1	GPIO Pin	Detects object presence
Proximity Sensor 2	GPIO Pin	Detects object presence
LED	GPIO Pin	Controlled based on sensor input

Connection Analysis

The proximity sensors detect objects and provide digital input signals to the microcontroller. The LED is connected to a GPIO pin and is controlled based on Boolean logic applied to the sensor inputs.

Program Software Setup

1. Open **Visual Studio Code** and create a new PlatformIO project.
2. Configure the GPIO pins for the proximity sensors and LED.
3. Implement code using Boolean operators to control the LED based on the sensor inputs.

Project Code

```c
#include <stdint.h>
#include <stdio.h>

#define LED_PIN 13          // GPIO pin for LED
#define SENSOR1_PIN 2       // GPIO pin for Proximity Sensor 1
#define SENSOR2_PIN 3       // GPIO pin for Proximity Sensor 2

void setup() {
    GPIO_DIR |= (1 << LED_PIN);       // Set LED pin as output
    GPIO_DIR &= ~(1 << SENSOR1_PIN);  // Set SENSOR1 pin as input
    GPIO_DIR &= ~(1 << SENSOR2_PIN);  // Set SENSOR2 pin as input
}

void controlLED(int sensor1, int sensor2) {
    // LED ON if both sensors detect an object
    if (sensor1 && sensor2) {
```

```
        GPIO_OUT |= (1 << LED_PIN); // Turn on LED
    }
    // LED ON if either sensor detects an object
    else if (sensor1 || sensor2) {
        GPIO_OUT |= (1 << LED_PIN); // Turn on LED
    }
    // Turn off LED if no sensor detects an object
    else {
        GPIO_OUT &= ~(1 << LED_PIN); // Turn off LED
    }
}

int main() {
    setup();

    while (1) {
        // Read sensor values
        int sensor1 = (GPIO_IN & (1 << SENSOR1_PIN)) != 0;
        int sensor2 = (GPIO_IN & (1 << SENSOR2_PIN)) != 0;

        controlLED(sensor1, sensor2); // Control LED based on sensor
inputs

        for (volatile int i = 0; i < 100000; i++); // Simple delay
    }
}
```

Save and Run

1. Save, compile, and upload the code to the **SiFive HiFive1 Rev B** board using PlatformIO.
2. Use the proximity sensors to test the LED behavior under different conditions.

Check Output

- The LED should turn on when both sensors detect an object (AND condition) or when either sensor detects an object (OR condition). If neither sensor detects an object, the LED remains off.

Compound Operators in C for RISC-V Microcontrollers

Chapter Overview
Compound operators in C combine arithmetic operations with assignment, allowing calculations and value updates in a single statement. These operators (+=, -=, *=, /=, %=, &=, |=, ^=) provide shorthand notation for common operations, improving code readability and efficiency. In embedded programming, compound operators are valuable for updating variables and controlling states in loops or conditional checks.

Chapter Goal

- Understand the primary compound operators and their functions in embedded C programming.
- Learn to use these operators to simplify code and improve efficiency.
- Implement a project using compound operators to adjust brightness levels of an LED using PWM.

Rules
- **Use Compound Operators for Efficiency**: Combine operations with assignment to minimize code length and improve readability.
- **Avoid Nested Compound Operations**: Use them in simple, clear expressions for better readability.
- **Check for Data Type Compatibility**: Ensure the data types are compatible with the operation to avoid unexpected results.
- **Avoid Overuse in Complex Expressions**: Keep compound operations straightforward to enhance maintainability.

Brief Introduction to Compound Operators
Compound operators simplify code by combining arithmetic, bitwise, and assignment operations. For example, x += 5 increments x by 5. These operators are essential for updating counters, toggling bits, and adjusting values in embedded systems. By using compound operators, programmers can make code more concise, especially in loops and repetitive operations.

Syntax Table

Serial No	Topic	Syntax	Simple Example
1	Addition	`a += b`	`counter += 1`
2	Subtraction	`a -= b`	`count -= decrement`
3	Multiplication	`a *= b`	`result *= factor`
4	Division	`a /= b`	`value /= divisor`
5	Modulus	`a %= b`	`remainder %= divisor`
6	Bitwise AND	`a &= b`	`flags &= mask`
8	Bitwise XOR	`a ^= b`	`toggle ^= 1`

Detailed Breakdown for Each Command

1. Addition Compound Operator (+=)

What is the Addition Compound Operator?

The += operator adds the right operand to the left operand and assigns the result to the left operand. It is commonly used for incrementing counters or adding values.

Use Purpose

- **Increment Values**: Simplifies incrementing variables in loops or counters.
- **Accumulate Totals**: Adds values to a running total, useful in data collection.

Syntax

```
a += b;
```

Syntax Explanation

- **a**: The variable being updated.
- **b**: The value to be added to a. The result is assigned back to a.

Simple Code Example

```
int counter = 0;
counter += 1;
```

Code Example Explanation

- Adds 1 to counter, which becomes 1.

Notes

- Equivalent to counter = counter + 1.

Warnings

- Be cautious with large additions to avoid overflow.

---

2. Subtraction Compound Operator (-=)

What is the Subtraction Compound Operator?

The -= operator subtracts the right operand from the left operand and assigns the result to the left operand. It is often used for decrementing values or reducing totals.

Use Purpose

- **Decrement Counters**: Efficiently decreases counters or values in loops.
- **Reduce Totals**: Subtracts values in accumulation tasks.

Syntax

```
a -= b;
```

Syntax Explanation

- **a**: The variable being updated.
- **b**: The value to be subtracted from a. The result is assigned back to a.

Simple Code Example

```
int count = 10;
count -= 2;
```

Code Example Explanation

- Subtracts 2 from count, resulting in 8.

Notes

- Equivalent to count = count - 2.

Warnings

- Avoid subtracting more than the current value in unsigned data types to prevent underflow.

---

3. Multiplication Compound Operator (*=)
What is the Multiplication Compound Operator?

The *= operator multiplies the left operand by the right operand and assigns the result to the left operand. It is useful for scaling values.

Use Purpose
- **Scaling**: Increases a variable by a multiplier.
- **Adjust Values**: Efficiently multiplies a variable in embedded calculations.

Syntax

```
a *= b;
```

Syntax Explanation

- **a**: The variable being updated.
- **b**: The value by which a is multiplied. The result is assigned back to a.

Simple Code Example

```
int result = 3;
result *= 4;
```

Code Example Explanation

- Multiplies `result` by 4, making it 12.

Notes

- Equivalent to `result` = `result` * 4.

Warnings

- Check for overflow in multiplication, especially with large integers.

---

4. Division Compound Operator (/=)

What is the Division Compound Operator?
The /= operator divides the left operand by the right operand and assigns the result to the left operand. It is commonly used to reduce values by a divisor.

Use Purpose

- **Scaling Down**: Reduces a value by dividing.
- **Average Calculations**: Useful in computing averages by dividing totals.

Syntax

```
a /= b;
```

Syntax Explanation

- **a**: The variable being updated.
- **b**: The divisor. The result is assigned back to a.

Simple Code Example

```
int value = 20;
value /= 4;
```

Code Example Explanation

- Divides `value` by 4, making it 5.

Notes

- Equivalent to `value = value / 4`.

Warnings

- Avoid division by zero, as it causes runtime errors.

---

5. Modulus Compound Operator (%=)

What is the Modulus Compound Operator?

The %= operator divides the left operand by the right operand and assigns the remainder to the left operand. It is used to keep values within a range.

Use Purpose

- **Cycle Management**: Keeps values within a specified boundary.
- **Odd/Even Checks**: Checks divisibility by obtaining remainders.

Syntax

```
a %= b;
```

Syntax Explanation

- **a**: The variable being updated.
- **b**: The divisor. The remainder is assigned back to a.

Simple Code Example

```
int remainder = 10;
remainder %= 3;
```

Code Example Explanation

- Divides remainder by 3, setting remainder to 1.

Notes

- Equivalent to remainder = remainder % 3.

Warnings

- Modulus is only valid for integer types and non-zero divisors.

---

6. Bitwise AND Compound Operator (&=)

What is the Bitwise AND Compound Operator?

The &= operator performs a bitwise AND operation between two values and assigns the result to the left operand. It is often used to mask bits.

Use Purpose

- **Masking**: Keeps specific bits in a value while clearing others.
- **Conditional Control**: Used in flag management in embedded systems.

Syntax

```
a &= b;
```

Syntax Explanation

- a: The variable being updated.
- b: The bitmask applied to a. The result is assigned back to a.

Simple Code Example

```
int flags = 0b1101;
flags &= 0b0101;
```

Code Example Explanation

- Sets `flags` to `0b0101` by masking with `0b0101`.

Notes

- Useful for preserving specific bits in a binary pattern.

Warnings

- Ensure the bitmask is correctly set to prevent unintended data loss.

---

7. Bitwise OR Compound Operator (|=)

What is the Bitwise OR Compound Operator?
The `|=` operator performs a bitwise OR operation, setting specific bits while keeping others unchanged. It is commonly used for setting flags.

Use Purpose

- **Flag Setting**: Activates specific bits without affecting others.
- **Feature Enabling**: Often used in control registers to enable specific features.

Syntax

```
a |= b;
```

Syntax Explanation

- **a**: The variable being updated.
- **b**: The bitmask applied to a. The result is assigned back to a.

Simple Code Example

```
int control = 0b0001;
control |= 0b0100;
```

Code Example Explanation

- Sets `control` to `0b0101` by applying a bitwise OR with `0b0100`.

Notes

- Maintains existing bits while setting specific ones.

Warnings

- Check bitmask values to avoid setting unintended bits.

---

8. Bitwise XOR Compound Operator (^=)

What is the Bitwise XOR Compound Operator?
The `^=` operator performs a bitwise XOR, toggling specified bits in the operand. It is often used for toggling features on and off.

Use Purpose

- **Toggle Bits**: Switches specific bits on and off.
- **Inversion Control**: Changes the state of specific bits without affecting others.

Syntax

```
a ^= b;
```

Syntax Explanation

- **a**: The variable being updated.
- **b**: The bitmask applied to a. The result is assigned back to a.

Simple Code Example

```
int toggle = 0b1010;
toggle ^= 0b1111;
```

Code Example Explanation

- Toggles bits in `toggle`, setting it to `0b0101`.

Notes

- XOR toggles bits, useful for reversible bit changes.

Relevant Project Section

Project Name
PWM-Based LED Brightness Control

Project Goal
Use compound operators on a RISC-V microcontroller to adjust the brightness of an LED using PWM, demonstrating compound operators' ability to update values and control hardware components.

RISC-V Development Environment
This project will use **PlatformIO** in **Visual Studio Code**.

RISC-V Microcontroller
We will use the **SiFive HiFive1 Rev B** microcontroller for this project.

Requirement Components

- **SiFive HiFive1 Rev B Microcontroller**
- **LED** connected to a PWM-capable GPIO pin

Component Connection Table

Component	RISC-V Pin	Additional Notes
LED	PWM Pin	Adjusts brightness via PWM duty cycle

Connection Analysis
The LED's brightness is controlled by adjusting the PWM duty cycle. The project uses compound operators to increase or decrease the duty cycle, allowing dynamic brightness control.

Program Software Setup

1. Open **Visual Studio Code** and create a new PlatformIO project.
2. Configure the PWM for LED control.
3. Implement code to adjust the PWM duty cycle using compound operators.

Project Code

```c
#include <stdint.h>
#include "hifive1_pwm.h"  // Include PWM library

#define LED_PIN 1          // PWM-capable pin for LED
#define STEP 10            // Increment/Decrement step for duty cycle

void setupPWM() {
    TIMER_INIT(1000);                // Initialize timer with 1 ms
period
    PWM_SET_DUTY(LED_PIN, 50);       // Start with 50% duty cycle
}

int main() {
    setupPWM();
    int dutyCycle = 50;              // Starting duty cycle

    while (1) {
        // Increase brightness
        if (dutyCycle <= 90) {
            dutyCycle += STEP;
        } else {
            dutyCycle -= STEP;       // Reduce brightness if limit is
reached
        }

        PWM_SET_DUTY(LED_PIN, dutyCycle); // Update PWM duty cycle

        for (volatile int i = 0; i < 100000; i++); // Simple delay
    }
}
```

Save and Run

1. Save, compile, and upload the code to the **SiFive HiFive1 Rev B** board using PlatformIO.
2. Observe the LED brightness increase and decrease, controlled by the PWM duty cycle adjustments.

Check Output

- The LED should gradually brighten and dim, showing compound operator usage to adjust the PWM duty cycle effectively.

Math Functions in C for RISC-V Microcontrollers

Chapter Overview

Math functions are essential in programming, enabling complex calculations, data processing, and manipulation of values. In embedded programming for RISC-V microcontrollers, math functions such as absolute value, power, square root, and trigonometric calculations enhance the ability to handle sensor data, perform mathematical modeling, and control outputs. This chapter will cover key math functions and demonstrate their application in an embedded project.

Chapter Goal

- Understand the main math functions (abs, pow, sqrt, etc.) and their applications in embedded C programming.
- Learn to use these functions effectively to handle sensor data and perform calculations.
- Implement a project that utilizes math functions to measure and display calculated values.

Rules

- **Use Math Functions Appropriately**: Select functions that match the data type and required precision.
- **Optimize for Performance**: Minimize the use of complex functions in time-sensitive code.
- **Be Aware of Floating-Point Usage**: Consider floating-point limitations, especially on embedded systems without hardware support.
- **Avoid Excessive Calculations in Loops**: For efficient code, calculate constants outside loops where possible.

Brief Introduction to Math Functions

Math functions perform essential calculations, such as finding the absolute value, power, square root, and trigonometric values. These functions allow microcontrollers to process data effectively, especially when working with sensor inputs that require scaling, normalization, or transformation.

Syntax Table

Serial No	Topic	Syntax	Simple Example
1	Absolute Value	`abs(x)`	`int result = abs(-5);`
2	Power	`pow(x, y)`	`double result = pow(2,3);`
3	Square Root	`sqrt(x)`	`double result = sqrt(16);`
4	Minimum Value	`fmin(x, y)`	`double minVal = fmin(5,3);`
5	Maximum Value	`fmax(x, y)`	`double maxVal = fmax(5,3);`

Detailed Breakdown for Each Command

1. Absolute Value (abs)

What is Absolute Value?
The abs function returns the non-negative value of an integer. It is often used to calculate distances or differences, ensuring the result is positive.

Use Purpose

- **Distance Calculations**: Provides the absolute difference between values.
- **Error Calculation**: Computes the magnitude of errors without regard to direction.

Syntax

```
abs(x);
```

Syntax Explanation

- **x**: The integer value whose absolute value is to be returned. If x is negative, it will be returned as positive.

Simple Code Example

```
int difference = abs(-10);
```

Code Example Explanation

- Converts -10 to 10, storing the result in `difference`.

Notes

- abs only works with integer values. For floating-point values, use `fabs()`.

Warnings

- Ensure that x is within the range of an integer to avoid overflow.

---

2. Power (pow)

What is Power?
The pow function calculates a base value raised to the power of an exponent. It is useful for exponential calculations, modeling, and scaling values.

Use Purpose

- **Exponential Scaling**: Applies exponential factors to data.
- **Modeling Calculations**: Frequently used in scientific and engineering formulas.

Syntax

```
pow(x, y);
```

Syntax Explanation

- **x**: The base value.
- **y**: The exponent. The result is x raised to the power of y.

Simple Code Example

```
double result = pow(2, 3);
```

Code Example Explanation

- Calculates 2 raised to the power of 3, giving 8.

Notes

- pow returns a floating-point result, so the output is of type double.

Warnings

- Avoid using high exponents with large bases, as this can lead to overflow.

---

3. Square Root (sqrt)
What is Square Root?
The sqrt function returns the square root of a number. It is useful for geometric calculations and data normalization.
Use Purpose
- **Distance Calculation**: Commonly used in distance and vector magnitude calculations.
- **Normalization**: Scales values by calculating the square root.
Syntax

```
sqrt(x);
```

Syntax Explanation

- **x**: The value whose square root is to be calculated. It must be non-negative.

Simple Code Example

```
double result = sqrt(16);
```

Code Example Explanation

- Calculates the square root of 16, which is 4.

Notes

- The argument must be non-negative; otherwise, it results in an error.

Warnings

- Avoid passing negative values to sqrt, as it can cause undefined behavior.

---

4. Minimum Value (fmin)

What is Minimum Value?

The fmin function returns the smaller of two floating-point values. It is often used in limit comparisons to select the lower bound.

Use Purpose

- **Lower Bound Selection**: Useful in finding the smaller limit in comparisons.
- **Data Comparison**: Selects the minimum of two values for data processing.

Syntax

```
fmin(x, y);
```

Syntax Explanation

- **x and y**: The two floating-point values being compared. The function returns the smaller of x and y.

Simple Code Example

```
double minVal = fmin(5.5, 3.3);
```

Code Example Explanation

- Returns 3.3 as the smaller value.

Notes

- For integer values, use the min function in custom logic.

Warnings

- Ensure inputs are valid floating-point values to avoid unexpected results.

---

5. Maximum Value (fmax)

What is Maximum Value?

The fmax function returns the larger of two floating-point values. It is useful in setting upper limits or selecting the larger of two values.

Use Purpose

- **Upper Bound Selection**: Finds the maximum of two values in control logic.
- **Data Thresholding**: Identifies maximum values for limit control.

Syntax

```
fmax(x, y);
```

Syntax Explanation

- **x and y**: The two floating-point values being compared. The function returns the larger of x and y.

Simple Code Example

```
double maxVal = fmax(5.5, 3.3);
```

Code Example Explanation

- Returns 5.5 as the larger value.

Notes

- Use fmax to simplify maximum comparison operations.

Warnings

- Check inputs to ensure compatibility with floating-point values.

Relevant Project Section

Project Name
Distance and Speed Calculation Using Math Functions

Project Goal
Use math functions on a RISC-V microcontroller to calculate distance and speed based on sensor data, demonstrating the practical use of sqrt and other math functions.

RISC-V Development Environment
This project will use **PlatformIO** in **Visual Studio Code**.

RISC-V Microcontroller
We will use the **SiFive HiFive1 Rev B** microcontroller for this project.

Requirement Components

- **SiFive HiFive1 Rev B Microcontroller**
- **Two Distance Sensors** connected to analog input pins
- **Display or Serial Output** for displaying calculated values

Component Connection Table

Component	RISC-V Pin	Additional Notes
Distance Sensor 1	ADC Pin	Provides first distance measurement
Distance Sensor 2	ADC Pin	Provides second distance measurement
Display/Serial Out	UART/Serial	Displays calculated speed and distance

Connection Analysis

The distance sensors provide analog signals representing measured distances. The microcontroller converts these signals to digital and uses math functions to calculate total distance and approximate speed based on measurements over time.

Program Software Setup

1. Open **Visual Studio Code** and create a new PlatformIO project.
2. Set up ADC to read data from the distance sensors.
3. Implement code to calculate the distance and speed using math functions such as sqrt and abs.

Project Code

```
#include <stdint.h>
#include <stdio.h>
#include <math.h>
#include "hifive1_adc.h"   // Include ADC library

#define SENSOR1_PIN 0           // ADC channel for sensor 1
#define SENSOR2_PIN 1           // ADC channel for sensor 2
#define TIME_INTERVAL 0.5       // Time interval in seconds

void setup() {
    ADC_INIT();                  // Initialize ADC
    ADC_SELECT_CHANNEL(SENSOR1_PIN);  // Set ADC channel for sensor 1
}

double calculateDistance(int sensor1Value, int sensor2Value) {
    // Using Pythagorean theorem as an example calculation
```

```c
    return sqrt(pow(sensor1Value, 2) + pow(sensor2Value, 2));
}

double calculateSpeed(double previousDistance, double currentDistance)
{
    double distanceDifference = fabs(currentDistance -
previousDistance);
    return distanceDifference / TIME_INTERVAL; // Speed = Distance /
Time
}

int main() {
    setup();
    double previousDistance = 0;

    while (1) {
        int sensor1Value = ADC_READ();          // Read from sensor 1
        ADC_SELECT_CHANNEL(SENSOR2_PIN);        // Switch to sensor 2
        int sensor2Value = ADC_READ();          // Read from sensor 2

        double currentDistance = calculateDistance(sensor1Value,
sensor2Value);
        double speed = calculateSpeed(previousDistance,
currentDistance);

        printf("Distance: %.2f units\n", currentDistance);
        printf("Speed: %.2f units/sec\n", speed);

        previousDistance = currentDistance;     // Update for next
calculation

        for (volatile int i = 0; i < 1000000; i++); // Simple delay
    }
}
```

Save and Run

1. Save, compile, and upload the code to the **SiFive HiFive1 Rev B** board using PlatformIO.
2. Observe the calculated distance and speed values displayed in the serial monitor.

Check Output

- The serial monitor should display updated distance and speed values based on the sensor inputs.

Characters in C for RISC-V Microcontrollers

Chapter Overview

Characters are fundamental data types in C that store single letters, digits, or symbols as numeric values using ASCII encoding. In embedded programming for RISC-V microcontrollers, characters are commonly used for processing text, displaying messages, and handling user inputs. This chapter will cover character data types, their usage, and how to manipulate characters in embedded applications.

Chapter Goal

- Understand character data types and how to work with them in C programming.
- Learn about key character functions and how to apply them in embedded applications.
- Implement a project that uses characters to display text and respond to user inputs.

Rules

- **Use Character Data Types for Single Symbols**: Use char when storing single characters rather than strings.
- **Convert Characters Appropriately**: Be mindful of uppercase and lowercase conversion when comparing characters.
- **Check ASCII Values**: Remember that characters are represented as integer values in ASCII encoding.
- **Avoid Using Characters in Mathematical Operations**: Limit characters to text handling for clarity and type safety.

Brief Introduction to Characters

Characters in C are stored as char data types and are represented as integers corresponding to ASCII codes. Characters are essential for handling text, displaying messages, and managing communication with text-based protocols. Common functions for handling characters include checking if a character is a letter or digit, converting to uppercase or lowercase, and comparing characters.

Syntax Table

Serial No	Topic	Syntax	Simple Example
1	Character Declaration	`char c`	`char letter = 'A';`
2	ASCII Value	`(int)char`	`int val = (int) 'A';`
3	Uppercase Conversion	`toupper(c)`	`char upper = toupper(c);`
4	Lowercase Conversion	`tolower(c)`	`char lower = tolower(c);`
5	Check Digit	`isdigit(c)`	`if (isdigit(c)) { }`

Detailed Breakdown for Each Command

1. Character Declaration (char)

What is Character Declaration?
The char type in C is used to store single characters. Each character corresponds to an integer value, typically based on the ASCII standard.

Use Purpose

- **Text Storage**: Store single letters, digits, or symbols.
- **Text-Based Communication**: Useful for handling character data in serial communication.

Syntax

```
char c;
```

Syntax Explanation

- **char**: Data type for storing a single character.
- **c**: Variable name representing the character.

Simple Code Example

```
char letter = 'A';
```

Code Example Explanation

- Declares a character variable `letter` and initializes it to 'A'.

Notes

- Characters are represented by their ASCII values internally, so 'A' corresponds to 65.

Warnings

- Ensure to use single quotes for character literals, as double quotes represent strings.

---

2. ASCII Value Conversion ((int)char)

What is ASCII Value Conversion?
Casting a character to an integer provides its ASCII value, enabling numeric comparisons or character manipulations based on ASCII codes.

Use Purpose

- **Character Comparison**: Allows comparison based on ASCII codes.
- **Text-Based Calculations**: Useful for offsetting or shifting characters.

Syntax

```
(int) char;
```

Syntax Explanation

- **(int)**: Casts the character to its integer ASCII representation.

Simple Code Example

```
int asciiValue = (int) 'A';
```

Code Example Explanation

- Converts the character 'A' to its ASCII integer value (65).

Notes

- ASCII codes for lowercase letters start at 97, and uppercase at 65.

Warnings

- Only valid for characters; casting non-character data may yield unexpected results.

---

3. Uppercase Conversion (toupper)

What is Uppercase Conversion?

The toupper function converts a lowercase letter to its uppercase equivalent if applicable.

Use Purpose

- **Uniform Case Handling**: Converts characters to uppercase for comparison.
- **Text Formatting**: Ensures consistency in displayed messages.

Syntax

```
toupper(c);
```

Syntax Explanation

- **c**: Character to convert to uppercase.

Simple Code Example

```
char upperLetter = toupper('b');
```

Code Example Explanation

- Converts 'b' to its uppercase version, 'B'.

Notes

- Only affects alphabetic characters; other characters remain unchanged.

Warnings

- Non-alphabetic characters should not be used with `toupper` as results are unpredictable.

---

4. Lowercase Conversion (`tolower`)

What is Lowercase Conversion?
The `tolower` function converts an uppercase letter to its lowercase equivalent if applicable.

Use Purpose

- **Text Consistency**: Converts characters to lowercase for consistent comparison.
- **User Input Handling**: Ensures user input is processed in a single case.

Syntax

```
tolower(c);
```

Syntax Explanation

- **c**: Character to convert to lowercase.

Simple Code Example

```
char lowerLetter = tolower('D');
```

Code Example Explanation

- Converts 'D' to its lowercase version, 'd'.

Notes

- Only alphabetic characters are affected.

Warnings

- Using `tolower` on non-alphabetic characters may yield unpredictable results.

---

5. Check Digit (`isdigit`)

What is Check Digit?
The `isdigit` function checks if a character represents a numeric digit (0-9). It is useful for input validation.

Use Purpose

- **Validation**: Ensures a character is a digit before performing operations.
- **Error Handling**: Checks user input or data received from sensors.

Syntax

```
isdigit(c);
```

Syntax Explanation

- **c**: Character to check if it's a digit.

Simple Code Example

```
if (isdigit('5')) {
    // Code executes if character is a digit
}
```

Code Example Explanation

- Checks if '5' is a digit; the condition is true.

Notes

- Only returns true for characters 0-9.

Warnings

- `isdigit` may not recognize non-ASCII numeric characters.

Relevant Project Section

Project Name
Serial Communication Text Display and Character Validation

Project Goal
Use character functions on a RISC-V microcontroller to display messages over serial communication and validate character inputs. This project demonstrates the practical use of character manipulation functions.

RISC-V Development Environment
This project will use **PlatformIO** in **Visual Studio Code**.

RISC-V Microcontroller
We will use the **SiFive HiFive1 Rev B** microcontroller for this project.

Requirement Components

- **SiFive HiFive1 Rev B Microcontroller**
- **Serial Communication Interface** for sending and receiving characters

Component Connection Table

Component	RISC-V Pin	Additional Notes
Serial Interface	UART Pins	Used to send and receive characters

Connection Analysis

This project will use the serial interface to display characters and validate input. The microcontroller will receive character input, validate if it's a digit, and convert characters to uppercase before displaying them.

Program Software Setup

1. Open **Visual Studio Code** and create a new PlatformIO project.
2. Set up serial communication for input and output.
3. Implement code that uses character functions to validate, convert, and display characters over the serial interface.

Project Code

```c
#include <stdint.h>
#include <stdio.h>
#include <ctype.h>

#define BAUD_RATE 9600  // Set appropriate baud rate

void setupSerial() {
    // Configure UART for serial communication (use RISC-V UART library
settings)
    UART_INIT(BAUD_RATE);
}

void processCharacter(char input) {
    if (isdigit(input)) {
        printf("'%c' is a digit.\n", input);
    } else {
        printf("'%c' is not a digit.\n", input);
    }

    char upper = toupper(input);
    char lower = tolower(input);

    printf("Uppercase: %c\n", upper);
    printf("Lowercase: %c\n", lower);
}

int main() {
    setupSerial();

    while (1) {
        char receivedChar;

        // Read a character from the serial input (simulate UART_READ)
        if (UART_AVAILABLE()) {
```

```
        receivedChar = UART_READ();

        // Process and display character details
        printf("Received: %c\n", receivedChar);
        processCharacter(receivedChar);
    }

    for (volatile int i = 0; i < 1000000; i++); // Simple delay
    }
}
```

Save and Run

1. Save, compile, and upload the code to the **SiFive HiFive1 Rev B** board using PlatformIO.
2. Use a serial terminal to send characters and observe the output for each character received.

Check Output

- The serial monitor should display whether each character is a digit and show its uppercase and lowercase forms.

Random Numbers in C for RISC-V Microcontrollers

Chapter Overview

Random numbers are essential for applications requiring variability, such as simulations, testing, games, and randomized responses. In embedded programming for RISC-V microcontrollers, random numbers can introduce randomness in control systems, data sampling, and security protocols. This chapter will cover random number generation techniques, their usage, and how to implement a random number-based project.

Chapter Goal

- Understand how to generate random numbers in C for RISC-V microcontrollers.
- Learn to seed and use random number functions for variability in embedded applications.
- Implement a project that uses random numbers to control LED patterns.

Rules

- **Seed Random Numbers for True Randomness**: Always use a unique seed to avoid repetitive results.
- **Avoid Using rand() in Time-Critical Code**: Generating random numbers can take time; avoid excessive use in critical sections.
- **Consider Hardware Limitations**: Some microcontrollers may lack support for complex random number generation; use software solutions accordingly.
- **Range Boundaries**: Ensure random values fall within the desired range to avoid out-of-bounds issues.

Brief Introduction to Random Numbers

Random number generation in C uses functions such as rand() to produce pseudo-random values. By default, rand() generates the same sequence each time, but by seeding it with srand(), you can create unique sequences. In embedded programming, random numbers add flexibility to applications, enabling varied responses, randomized events, and testing scenarios.

Syntax Table

Serial No	Topic	Syntax	Simple Example
1	Seed Randomizer	`srand(seed);`	`srand(analogRead(pin));`
2	Generate Random	`rand()`	`int num = rand();`
3	Random Range	`rand() % range`	`int num = rand() % 10;`

Detailed Breakdown for Each Command

1. Seed Randomizer (srand)

What is Seed Randomizer?
The srand function seeds the random number generator, setting the starting point for the sequence of random values. Without seeding, rand() produces the same sequence on every run.

Use Purpose

- **Ensure Variability**: Seeds the random number generator for unique random sequences.
- **Enhanced Randomness**: Adding a seed, like a sensor reading, ensures unpredictable results.

Syntax

```
srand(seed);
```

Syntax Explanation

- **seed**: An integer value used to initialize the random number generator. Typically, a dynamic value (e.g., sensor reading) is used for unique results.

Simple Code Example

```
srand(analogRead(A0));   // Use an analog sensor reading as a seed
```

Code Example Explanation

- Seeds the random number generator with an analog sensor reading to create unique random values.

Notes

- Seeding with the same value each time generates the same random sequence.

Warnings

- Avoid using fixed values as seeds unless repeatability is desired.

---

2. Generate Random (rand)

What is Generate Random?

The rand() function returns a pseudo-random integer between 0 and RAND_MAX. It produces a sequence of values based on the initial seed.

Use Purpose

- **Generate Random Values**: Creates pseudo-random numbers for varied behavior.
- **Simulation and Testing**: Useful for randomized input simulation in testing environments.

Syntax

```
rand();
```

Syntax Explanation

- **rand()**: The function call generates a pseudo-random integer between 0 and RAND_MAX.

Simple Code Example

```
int num = rand();
```

Code Example Explanation

- Generates a random integer and stores it in num.

Notes

- For specific ranges, use modulus (%) to limit rand() output.

Warnings

- rand() is pseudo-random; it provides predictable results without seeding.

---

3. Random Range (rand() % range)

What is Random Range?
Using rand() % range limits the output of rand() to a specific range. This operation returns a value from 0 up to range - 1.

Use Purpose

- **Controlled Randomization**: Constrains random values within desired limits, ideal for LED patterns, motor speeds, or timings.
- **Custom Range Control**: Useful for setting boundaries on random numbers.

Syntax

```
rand() % range;
```

Syntax Explanation

- **rand()**: Generates a pseudo-random integer.
- **% range**: Limits the random integer to values between 0 and range - 1.

Simple Code Example

```
int randomLED = rand() % 5;   // Generates a random number from 0 to 4
```

Code Example Explanation

- Generates a random value between 0 and 4, suitable for selecting one of five LEDs.

Notes

- Ensure that range is greater than 0 to avoid division by zero.

Warnings

- Using % on rand() reduces randomness slightly but is generally acceptable for bounded values.

Relevant Project Section

Project Name
Random LED Pattern Generator

Project Goal
Use random numbers on a RISC-V microcontroller to control the lighting of LEDs in a random pattern. This project demonstrates the use of rand() and srand() to generate random values for embedded applications.

RISC-V Development Environment
This project will use **PlatformIO** in **Visual Studio Code**.
RISC-V Microcontroller
We will use the **SiFive HiFive1 Rev B** microcontroller for this project.
Requirement Components

- **SiFive HiFive1 Rev B Microcontroller**
- **5 LEDs** connected to GPIO pins for random activation

Component Connection Table

Component	RISC-V Pin	Additional Notes
LED1	GPIO Pin 2	LED for random activation
LED2	GPIO Pin 3	LED for random activation
LED3	GPIO Pin 4	LED for random activation
LED4	GPIO Pin 5	LED for random activation
LED5	GPIO Pin 6	LED for random activation

Connection Analysis

Each LED is connected to a separate GPIO pin, allowing the microcontroller to control individual LEDs. Random numbers determine which LEDs are activated at any given time, creating a random light pattern.

Program Software Setup

1. Open **Visual Studio Code** and create a new PlatformIO project.
2. Set up the GPIO pins for each LED.
3. Implement code to seed the random number generator and activate random LEDs using `rand()`.

Project Code

```
#include <stdint.h>
#include <stdio.h>
#include <stdlib.h>
#include "hifive1_gpio.h"   // GPIO library for RISC-V

#define NUM_LEDS 5
int ledPins[NUM_LEDS] = {2, 3, 4, 5, 6};   // Array of LED GPIO pins

void setup() {
    // Initialize each LED pin as output
```

```c
    for (int i = 0; i < NUM_LEDS; i++) {
        GPIO_DIR |= (1 << ledPins[i]);
    }

    // Seed the random number generator
    srand(analogRead(0));  // Use an analog reading as seed
}

void randomLEDPattern() {
    int randomLED = rand() % NUM_LEDS;  // Select random LED

    // Turn all LEDs off
    for (int i = 0; i < NUM_LEDS; i++) {
        GPIO_OUT &= ~(1 << ledPins[i]);
    }

    // Turn on the randomly selected LED
    GPIO_OUT |= (1 << ledPins[randomLED]);
}

int main() {
    setup();

    while (1) {
        randomLEDPattern();  // Activate random LED pattern

        for (volatile int i = 0; i < 1000000; i++);  // Simple delay
    }
}
```

Save and Run

1. Save, compile, and upload the code to the **SiFive HiFive1 Rev B** board using PlatformIO.
2. Observe the LED lights activate in random patterns, controlled by the microcontroller.

Check Output

- The LEDs should light up in a random sequence, with only one LED active at a time.

Time and Counting in C for RISC-V Microcontrollers

Chapter Overview

Time and counting are fundamental in embedded programming, allowing microcontrollers to manage delays, measure durations, and control time-based events. In RISC-V microcontrollers, these operations are essential for tasks like generating PWM signals, controlling motors, blinking LEDs, and creating precise timing mechanisms. This chapter will cover basic time and counting functions, the syntax of time-related commands, and their applications in embedded projects.

Chapter Goal

- Understand the use of time functions and counting loops in embedded C programming.
- Learn to implement delays, count events, and manage time-based actions effectively.
- Implement a project that uses time and counting to create an LED blink sequence with precise timing.

Rules

- **Avoid Blocking Delays**: Use non-blocking delay methods in critical systems to avoid slowing down other operations.
- **Consider Timer Accuracy**: Be mindful of the timer's accuracy for applications requiring precise timing.
- **Optimize Time-Intensive Loops**: Minimize complex calculations within time loops to maintain efficiency.
- **Use Hardware Timers for Accuracy**: For more accurate timing, consider using the microcontroller's hardware timers.

Brief Introduction to Time and Counting

Time and counting functions in C help microcontrollers manage delays and execute time-based tasks. Using delay loops and timers, microcontrollers can control the duration of events, create periodic actions, and measure elapsed time. Common time functions include delay, millis, and counters to increment values over time.

Syntax Table

Serial No	Topic	Syntax	Simple Example
1	Delay Loop	`for` loop	`for (i=0; i<delay; i++);`
2	Milliseconds	`millis()`	`unsigned long time = millis();`
3	Hardware Timer	`timer_init()`	`timer_init(1000);`
4	Event Counter	`counter++`	`eventCounter++;`
5	Delay Function	`delay(ms)`	`delay(1000);`

Detailed Breakdown for Each Command

1. Delay Loop (`for` loop)
What is Delay Loop?
A `for` loop can create a delay by counting up to a specific number, creating a software delay without relying on hardware timers.

Use Purpose
- **Simple Delays**: Implements basic delays in embedded programs.
- **Non-Critical Delays**: Useful in non-time-sensitive applications.

Syntax

```
for (int i = 0; i < delay; i++);
```

Syntax Explanation
- **i**: Counter variable that iterates until it reaches delay.
- **delay**: Represents the number of loop iterations, controlling delay duration.

Simple Code Example

```
for (int i = 0; i < 100000; i++);
```

Code Example Explanation

- Creates a delay by counting up to 100000, pausing program execution momentarily.

Notes

- Delay duration is approximate and depends on the clock speed.

Warnings

- Avoid large delays within critical sections to maintain program responsiveness.

---

2. Milliseconds (`millis`)

What is Milliseconds?
The `millis` function returns the number of milliseconds since the program started. It's commonly used to track elapsed time or schedule periodic tasks.

Use Purpose

- **Event Scheduling**: Tracks time for repeating events.
- **Elapsed Time Measurement**: Measures the duration between events.

Syntax

```
millis();
```

Syntax Explanation

- **`millis()`**: Returns an unsigned long representing the milliseconds elapsed since the program started.

Simple Code Example

```
unsigned long startTime = millis();
```

Code Example Explanation

- Stores the current time in `startTime` to track the beginning of an event.

Notes

- `millis()` typically rolls over after reaching the maximum unsigned long value.

Warnings

- Be cautious with rollover if the program runs for extended periods.

---

3. Hardware Timer (`timer_init`)

What is Hardware Timer?

`timer_init` initializes a hardware timer with a specified frequency, offering accurate timing without blocking the CPU. Hardware timers are essential for PWM, precise delays, and periodic interrupts.

Use Purpose

- **Accurate Timing**: Generates precise time intervals.
- **Periodic Actions**: Triggers recurring actions, like reading sensors.

Syntax

```
timer_init(frequency);
```

Syntax Explanation

- **`frequency`**: Sets the timer's frequency, defining how often it triggers.

Simple Code Example

```
timer_init(1000);  // Sets timer to 1kHz
```

Code Example Explanation

- Configures the timer to trigger at 1kHz, useful for 1ms periodic tasks.

Notes

- Hardware timers operate independently, providing accurate timing.

Warnings

- Ensure proper timer initialization to avoid conflicts with other processes.

---

4. Event Counter (counter++)

What is Event Counter?

The counter++ syntax increments a counter variable, commonly used to count events or occurrences.

Use Purpose

- **Event Counting**: Counts the number of times an event occurs.
- **Loop Control**: Manages iterations within a loop.

Syntax

```
counter++;
```

Syntax Explanation

- **counter**: The variable that increments by 1 each time it is accessed.

Simple Code Example

```
int eventCounter = 0;
eventCounter++;
```

Code Example Explanation

- Increments `eventCounter` by 1, tracking the number of events.

Notes

- Counter variables can be reset as needed to restart the count.

Warnings

- Prevent overflow by choosing an appropriate data type, such as `unsigned int`.

---

5. Delay Function (`delay`)

What is Delay Function?
The `delay` function pauses program execution for a specified number of milliseconds. It provides a simple, blocking delay that's useful in basic timing control.

Use Purpose

- **Fixed Duration Delay**: Pauses the program temporarily.
- **Timing Control**: Controls the duration of operations, like LED blink rate.

Syntax

```
delay(ms);
```

Syntax Explanation

- **ms**: The delay duration in milliseconds.

Simple Code Example

```
delay(1000);  // 1-second delay
```

Code Example Explanation

- Pauses program execution for 1 second.

Notes

- Delay function blocks other tasks; avoid in critical applications.

Warnings

- Blocking delays halt program execution; use sparingly in time-sensitive systems.

Relevant Project Section
Project Name
LED Blink Sequence with Precise Timing
Project Goal
Use time and counting functions on a RISC-V microcontroller to create an LED blink sequence with controlled timing. This project demonstrates basic delay functions, event counters, and hardware timers to control LED behavior.
RISC-V Development Environment
This project will use **PlatformIO** in **Visual Studio Code**.
RISC-V Microcontroller
We will use the **SiFive HiFive1 Rev B** microcontroller for this project.
Requirement Components
- **SiFive HiFive1 Rev B Microcontroller**
- **LED** connected to a GPIO pin for timing control

Component Connection Table

Component	RISC-V Pin	Additional Notes
LED	GPIO Pin 2	Controls LED timing

Connection Analysis

The LED is connected to a GPIO pin. Using time functions, the microcontroller controls the LED blink interval, creating a sequence with a precise timing pattern.

Program Software Setup

1. Open **Visual Studio Code** and create a new PlatformIO project.
2. Set up the GPIO pin for the LED.
3. Implement code using delays, counters, and timers to create a blink sequence.

Project Code

```c
#include <stdint.h>
#include <stdio.h>

#define LED_PIN 2                // GPIO pin for LED
#define BLINK_INTERVAL 1000      // 1-second blink interval
void setup() {
    GPIO_DIR |= (1 << LED_PIN); // Set LED pin as output
}
void blinkLED() {
    GPIO_OUT ^= (1 << LED_PIN); // Toggle LED state
}

int main() {
    setup();
    unsigned long previousMillis = 0;

    while (1) {
        unsigned long currentMillis = millis();

        // Check if the interval has passed
        if (currentMillis - previousMillis >= BLINK_INTERVAL) {
            previousMillis = currentMillis;  // Update previous time
            blinkLED();                      // Toggle LED state
        }
    }
}
```

Save and Run

1. Save, compile, and upload the code to the **SiFive HiFive1 Rev B** board using PlatformIO.
2. Observe the LED blinking at 1-second intervals, controlled by the timer-based delay.

Check Output

- The LED should blink on and off at 1-second intervals, demonstrating precise timing using the `millis()` function.

Data Conversion in C for RISC-V Microcontrollers

Chapter Overview

Data conversion is crucial in embedded programming, enabling microcontrollers to transform data from one format to another, such as from integers to floating-point or from analog to digital values. In RISC-V microcontrollers, data conversion is frequently needed to process sensor data, communicate values, and perform mathematical operations. This chapter will cover various data conversion techniques, syntax, and their applications in embedded projects.

Chapter Goal

- Understand common data conversion techniques and their usage in C programming for embedded applications.
- Learn to implement typecasting, analog-to-digital conversions, and conversions between different number bases.
- Implement a project that converts and displays sensor data in multiple formats.

Rules

- **Match Data Types Carefully**: Ensure compatibility between data types during conversion to avoid data loss or overflow.
- **Use Conversions for Meaningful Data**: Convert data for meaningful processing, such as analog-to-digital conversions for sensors.
- **Check for Overflow and Underflow**: Avoid exceeding data type limits during conversion to maintain accuracy.
- **Convert in a Stepwise Manner**: For complex conversions, break them down into intermediate steps to improve readability and accuracy.

Brief Introduction to Data Conversion

Data conversion in embedded C includes techniques such as typecasting (changing data from one type to another), base conversion (converting values from one numeral system to another), and analog-to-digital conversions (transforming sensor signals into readable digital data). Conversions are essential in ensuring compatibility between different data types and formats, making the data usable in various contexts.

Syntax Table

Serial No	Topic	Syntax	Simple Example
1	Typecasting	`(type) value`	`float f = (float) 10;`
2	Integer to Float	`(float) intVar`	`float result = (float) num;`
3	Float to Integer	`(int) floatVar`	`int rounded = (int) value;`
4	ASCII to Integer	`atoi(string)`	`int num = atoi("123");`
5	Integer to String	`itoa(int, str, base)`	`itoa(num, str, 10);`

Detailed Breakdown for Each Command

1. Typecasting (`(type) value`)

What is Typecasting?

Typecasting converts a variable from one data type to another, allowing data to be interpreted differently. This is especially useful when performing calculations that require different data types, such as converting integer sensor readings to floating-point for precision.

Use Purpose

- **Data Compatibility**: Ensures compatibility in operations involving different data types.
- **Precision Control**: Allows converting integer values to floating-point for increased precision.

Syntax

```
(type) value;
```

Syntax Explanation

- **type**: The target data type to which `value` will be converted.
- **value**: The variable or value being typecast.

Simple Code Example

```
float f = (float) 10;   // Converts integer 10 to float
```

Code Example Explanation

- Converts the integer 10 to a floating-point value, storing 10.0 in f.

Notes

- Typecasting allows mixing of data types within expressions.

Warnings

- Avoid losing data through typecasting, such as truncating decimals when converting float to int.

---

2. Integer to Float Conversion ((`float`) `intVar`)

What is Integer to Float Conversion?

Converting an integer to a float enables precise calculations by adding decimal representation, useful when exact values are required, such as in sensor calibration.

Use Purpose

- **Enhanced Precision**: Provides decimal accuracy for mathematical operations.
- **Sensor Data Processing**: Converts integer sensor data to float for accurate processing.

Syntax

```
(float) intVar;
```

Syntax Explanation

- **intVar**: The integer variable being converted to float.

Simple Code Example

```
int num = 7;
float preciseNum = (float) num;
```

Code Example Explanation

- Converts the integer 7 to 7.0 as a float.

Notes

- Integer-to-float conversions are commonly used in averaging and scaling operations.

Warnings

- Be mindful of decimal precision requirements when converting large numbers.

---

3. Float to Integer Conversion ((int) floatVar)

What is Float to Integer Conversion?

Float-to-integer conversion discards the decimal portion of a floating-point value, useful when only the whole number is needed, such as in counters or non-fractional values.

Use Purpose

- **Whole Number Processing**: Simplifies values by removing decimals.
- **Data Formatting**: Converts precise data to whole numbers for simplified display.

Syntax

```
(int) floatVar;
```

Syntax Explanation

- **floatVar**: The floating-point variable being converted to an integer.

Simple Code Example

```
float value = 9.7;
int rounded = (int) value;   // Converts to 9
```

Code Example Explanation

- Converts 9.7 to 9, discarding the decimal part.

Notes

- Rounding is not applied; values are truncated to integers.

Warnings

- Be cautious when truncating values; decimals will be lost permanently.

---

4. ASCII to Integer Conversion (atoi)

What is ASCII to Integer Conversion?

The atoi function converts a string of ASCII characters to an integer, enabling the use of numerical data input from character-based sources, like serial data.

Use Purpose

- **Text-Based Input**: Converts numerical text inputs to integer format.
- **Serial Data Processing**: Useful for interpreting numerical strings from serial communication.

Syntax

```
atoi(string);
```

Syntax Explanation

- **string**: A character array or string containing numeric ASCII characters to be converted.

Simple Code Example

```
int num = atoi("123");
```

Code Example Explanation

- Converts the string "123" to the integer 123.

Notes

- Ensure the string contains valid numeric characters to avoid errors.

Warnings

- atoi returns 0 for invalid strings; validate inputs when necessary.

---

5. Integer to String Conversion (itoa)

What is Integer to String Conversion?

The itoa function converts an integer to a string in a specified numeral base, useful for displaying numbers or sending them as text over communication protocols.

Use Purpose

- **Data Display**: Formats integer values as strings for display purposes.
- **Communication**: Sends integer data as strings in serial communication.

Syntax

```
itoa(int, str, base);
```

Syntax Explanation

- `int`: The integer value to be converted.
- `str`: The destination character array for the resulting string.
- `base`: Specifies the numeral system (e.g., 10 for decimal).

Simple Code Example

```
char buffer[10];
itoa(123, buffer, 10);   // Converts 123 to "123" in decimal
```

Code Example Explanation

- Converts the integer 123 to the string "123" in decimal format.

Notes

- Buffer size must be large enough to store the resulting string.

Warnings

- Incorrect buffer sizes can lead to memory issues; ensure adequate storage.

Relevant Project Section

Project Name
Sensor Data Conversion and Display

Project Goal

Use data conversion functions on a RISC-V microcontroller to process and display analog sensor data in multiple formats. This project demonstrates integer-to-float, float-to-integer, and ASCII conversions.

RISC-V Development Environment

This project will use **PlatformIO** in **Visual Studio Code**.

RISC-V Microcontroller

We will use the **SiFive HiFive1 Rev B** microcontroller for this project.

Requirement Components

- **SiFive HiFive1 Rev B Microcontroller**
- **Analog Temperature Sensor** connected to an ADC pin
- **Serial Communication Interface** for displaying converted values

Component Connection Table

Component	RISC-V Pin	Additional Notes
Temperature Sensor	ADC Pin	Provides analog voltage based on temp
Serial Interface	UART Pins	Displays converted sensor values

Connection Analysis

The temperature sensor provides an analog voltage proportional to temperature. The microcontroller reads this analog value, converts it to digital, and applies data conversions to display results as integers, floats, and ASCII strings over serial communication.

Program Software Setup

1. Open **Visual Studio Code** and create a new PlatformIO project.
2. Configure the ADC for reading sensor data and set up UART for serial output.

3. Implement code to read, convert, and display sensor data in various formats.

Project Code

```c
#include <stdint.h>
#include <stdio.h>
#include <stdlib.h>

#define ADC_PIN 0   // ADC channel for temperature sensor

void setup() {
    ADC_INIT();                 // Initialize ADC
    UART_INIT(9600);            // Initialize UART for serial output
}

void displaySensorData(int adcValue) {
    float temperature = (float)adcValue * (3.3 / 1023.0) * 100;  //
Convert ADC to Celsius
    int integerTemp = (int)temperature;                          //
Float to integer
    char tempString[10];
    itoa(integerTemp, tempString, 10);                           //
Integer to string

    printf("Analog Value: %d\n", adcValue);
    printf("Temperature (float): %.2f°C\n", temperature);
    printf("Temperature (integer): %d°C\n", integerTemp);
    printf("Temperature (string): %s°C\n", tempString);
}

int main() {
    setup();

    while (1) {
        int adcValue = ADC_READ();          // Read analog value from
sensor
        displaySensorData(adcValue);        // Display converted values

        for (volatile int i = 0; i < 1000000; i++);   // Simple delay
    }
}
```

Save and Run

1. Save, compile, and upload the code to the **SiFive HiFive1 Rev B** board using PlatformIO.
2. Monitor the serial output to observe the sensor data in different formats.

Check Output

- The serial monitor should display the sensor's ADC value, floating-point temperature, integer temperature, and temperature as a string.

Functions in C for RISC-V Microcontrollers

Chapter Overview

Functions are essential in C programming, allowing code to be organized, reused, and modularized. In embedded programming on RISC-V microcontrollers, functions enable efficient code management, making it easier to handle tasks like reading sensors, controlling outputs, and processing data. Functions improve readability, reduce redundancy, and simplify debugging.

Chapter Goal

- Understand the purpose and structure of functions in embedded C programming.
- Learn to define and use functions for various tasks, such as data processing and hardware control.
- Implement a project that uses functions to read sensor data and control an LED based on thresholds.

Rules

- **Define Functions for Reusable Code**: Use functions to encapsulate repeated code, making it reusable and modular.
- **Keep Functions Simple**: Each function should perform one specific task to maintain clarity.
- **Use Descriptive Names**: Name functions based on their purpose for easy understanding.
- **Limit Global Variables**: Pass data as function arguments to reduce reliance on global variables and increase flexibility.

Brief Introduction to Functions

A function in C is a block of code designed to perform a specific task. Functions have a name, return type, and parameters, enabling them to operate on given inputs and return a result. Functions make code more readable and maintainable, which is crucial in embedded systems where complex tasks are broken down into smaller operations.

Syntax Table

Serial No	Topic	Syntax	Simple Example
1	Function Declaration	`returnType functionName(parameters);`	`int add(int, int);`
2	Function Definition	`returnType functionName(parameters) { ... }`	`int add(int a, int b) { return a + b; }`
3	Function Call	`functionName(arguments);`	`int sum = add(5, 3);`
4	Return Statement	`return value;`	`return a + b;`
5	Void Function	`void functionName()`	`void blinkLED();`

Detailed Breakdown for Each Command

1. Function Declaration
What is Function Declaration?
A function declaration specifies the function's name, return type, and parameters without providing its actual code. It tells the compiler that the function exists and defines its usage format.
Use Purpose
- **Declare Functions for Later Use**: Allows functions to be used before they are defined in the code.
- **Define Function Interface**: Provides the structure of the function, specifying input and output.

Syntax

```
returnType functionName(parameters);
```

Syntax Explanation

- **returnType**: Specifies the data type of the value the function will return (e.g., `int`, `float`, `void`).
- **functionName**: The name of the function, which is used to call it.
- **parameters**: Data types and names of the inputs the function accepts.

Simple Code Example

```
int add(int a, int b);
```

Code Example Explanation

- Declares a function named add that takes two integers as parameters and returns an integer.

Notes

- Declarations are usually placed at the beginning of the code or in header files.

Warnings

- Ensure that parameters match between the declaration and the function definition.

---

2. Function Definition
What is Function Definition?
A function definition provides the actual code for a function, including the instructions executed when the function is called.
Use Purpose
- **Provide Function Logic**: Defines the operations to perform when the function is called.
- **Encapsulate Code**: Allows a specific task to be grouped and reused.

Syntax

```
returnType functionName(parameters) {
    // Code to execute
}
```

Syntax Explanation

- **returnType**: Specifies the function's return data type.
- **functionName**: The name used to call the function.
- **parameters**: Specifies input data types and names.
- **Code Block**: The instructions executed within the function.

Simple Code Example

```
int add(int a, int b) {
    return a + b;
}
```

Code Example Explanation

- Defines the function add, which returns the sum of two integers, a and b.

Notes

- Functions can return data or be void, returning no value.

Warnings

- Be consistent with the data types specified in the declaration.

---

3. Function Call
What is Function Call?
A function call invokes a function by its name, passing any required arguments, and executes its code.
Use Purpose
- **Execute Function Code**: Triggers the function to perform its defined task.
- **Reusability**: Calls the same function multiple times with different arguments.

Syntax

```
functionName(arguments);
```

Syntax Explanation

- **functionName**: The name of the function to execute.
- **arguments**: The values passed to the function's parameters.

Simple Code Example

```
int sum = add(5, 3);
```

Code Example Explanation

- Calls the add function with arguments 5 and 3, storing the result in sum.

Notes

- Functions can be called from other functions, including main.

Warnings

- Ensure arguments match parameter types to avoid unexpected results.

---

4. Return Statement

What is Return Statement?

The return statement specifies the value a function sends back to the caller. In non-void functions, it concludes the function's execution.

Use Purpose

- **Provide Function Output**: Delivers a result back to the caller.
- **Exit Function**: Ends the function's execution.

Syntax

```
return value;
```

Syntax Explanation

- **value**: The data sent back to the caller, matching the function's return type.

Simple Code Example

```
return a + b;
```

Code Example Explanation

- Returns the sum of a and b as the function's result.

Notes

- Void functions omit the `return` keyword or use `return;` without a value.

Warnings

- Ensure the returned value matches the declared return type.

---

5. Void Function

What is Void Function?
A void function performs tasks but does not return a value. It's useful for actions that don't require feedback, such as LED control or printing messages.

Use Purpose
- **Perform Actions**: Executes code without returning a result.
- **Hardware Control**: Ideal for tasks like blinking an LED or turning on a motor.

Syntax

```
void functionName() {
    // Code to execute
}
```

Syntax Explanation

- **void**: Specifies that the function does not return any value.

Simple Code Example

```
void blinkLED() {
    // Toggle LED
}
```

Code Example Explanation

- Defines a function `blinkLED` that controls the LED without returning a value.

Notes

- Void functions are commonly used for I/O operations in embedded systems.

Warnings

- Void functions cannot return a value.

Relevant Project Section

Project Name
Sensor-Based LED Control with Functions

Project Goal
Use functions on a RISC-V microcontroller to read a sensor value and control an LED based on thresholds. This project demonstrates how functions organize code, making it modular and reusable.

RISC-V Development Environment
This project will use **PlatformIO** in **Visual Studio Code**.

RISC-V Microcontroller
We will use the **SiFive HiFive1 Rev B** microcontroller for this project.

Requirement Components

- **SiFive HiFive1 Rev B Microcontroller**
- **Analog Temperature Sensor** connected to an ADC pin
- **LED** connected to a GPIO pin to indicate temperature range

Component Connection Table

Component	RISC-V Pin	Additional Notes
Temperature Sensor	ADC Pin	Provides analog temperature data
LED	GPIO Pin	Turns on if temperature exceeds threshold

Connection Analysis

The temperature sensor provides an analog value representing temperature. A function reads this value, converts it, and another function controls the LED based on temperature thresholds.

Program Software Setup

1. Open **Visual Studio Code** and create a new PlatformIO project.
2. Set up the ADC for sensor reading and the GPIO pin for the LED.
3. Implement functions for reading sensor data, converting values, and controlling the LED.

Project Code

```
#include <stdint.h>
#include <stdio.h>

#define LED_PIN 2                // GPIO pin for LED
#define TEMP_THRESHOLD 30        // Temperature threshold in Celsius

void setup() {
    GPIO_DIR |= (1 << LED_PIN); // Set LED pin as output
    ADC_INIT();                 // Initialize ADC for sensor reading
}

// Function to read the sensor and convert to Celsius
```

```c
float readTemperature() {
    int adcValue = ADC_READ();
    float voltage = (adcValue / 1023.0) * 3.3;
    return voltage * 100;  // Convert voltage to temperature (example)
}

// Function to control LED based on temperature
void controlLED(float temperature) {
    if (temperature >= TEMP_THRESHOLD) {
        GPIO_OUT |= (1 << LED_PIN);   // Turn LED on
    } else {
        GPIO_OUT &= ~(1 << LED_PIN); // Turn LED off
    }
}

int main() {
    setup();

    while (1) {
        float temperature = readTemperature(); // Read temperature
        controlLED(temperature);                // Control LED based on
temperature

        for (volatile int i = 0; i < 1000000; i++);  // Simple delay
    }
}
```

Save and Run

1. Save, compile, and upload the code to the **SiFive HiFive1 Rev B** board using PlatformIO.
2. Observe the LED, which turns on when the temperature exceeds the threshold.

Check Output

- The LED should turn on when the temperature is above the threshold and turn off when below.

Power Management in RISC-V Microcontrollers

Chapter Overview

Power management is essential in embedded systems, particularly for applications that run on batteries or have strict energy constraints. By reducing power consumption, microcontrollers can extend battery life, lower heat production, and improve efficiency. RISC-V microcontrollers offer various power management features such as sleep modes, low-power modes, and peripheral control. This chapter will cover common power management techniques, their syntax, and practical applications in embedded projects.

Chapter Goal

- Understand power management modes and functions available in RISC-V microcontrollers.
- Learn how to implement low-power techniques to optimize power consumption.
- Implement a project to use sleep modes and wake up the microcontroller on an external event.

Rules

- **Use Low-Power Modes When Idle**: Engage sleep modes when the microcontroller is not performing critical tasks.
- **Disable Unused Peripherals**: Turn off peripherals that are not required to conserve power.
- **Optimize Wake-Up Events**: Configure the microcontroller to wake up only on essential events.
- **Monitor Battery Levels**: In battery-powered applications, track battery levels and adjust power settings accordingly.

Brief Introduction to Power Management

Power management functions allow the microcontroller to save energy by entering low-power states, such as sleep modes, where it uses minimal power. Different sleep modes offer various levels of power savings and operational states. Microcontrollers can also selectively enable or disable peripherals, ensuring that only necessary components consume power.

Syntax Table

Serial No	Topic	Syntax	Simple Example
1	Enter Sleep Mode	`enter_sleep_mode();`	`enter_sleep_mode();`
2	Wake-Up Source	`set_wakeup_source(pin);`	`set_wakeup_source(PIN2);`
3	Disable Peripheral	`disable_peripheral(name);`	`disable_peripheral(UART);`
4	Enable Peripheral	`enable_peripheral(name);`	`enable_peripheral(UART);`
5	Sleep for Duration	`sleep(duration);`	`sleep(500);`

Detailed Breakdown for Each Command

1. Enter Sleep Mode (`enter_sleep_mode`)

What is Enter Sleep Mode?
The `enter_sleep_mode` function puts the microcontroller into a low-power state, where it consumes minimal power but retains the ability to wake up on specific events.

Use Purpose

- **Reduce Power Usage**: Minimizes energy consumption when the system is idle.
- **Extend Battery Life**: Critical for battery-powered applications to save energy.

Syntax

```
enter_sleep_mode();
```

Syntax Explanation

- **`enter_sleep_mode`**: Function call that sends the microcontroller into its designated low-power sleep mode.

Simple Code Example

```
enter_sleep_mode();
```

Code Example Explanation

- Puts the microcontroller into sleep mode, reducing power consumption until a wake-up event occurs.

Notes

- The specific behavior depends on the configured sleep mode and wake-up sources.

Warnings

- Ensure wake-up sources are configured; otherwise, the microcontroller may remain in sleep mode indefinitely.

---

2. Wake-Up Source (`set_wakeup_source`)

What is Wake-Up Source?

The `set_wakeup_source` function defines which external event, such as a pin change or timer, can wake up the microcontroller from sleep mode.

Use Purpose

- **Wake Up on Specific Events**: Configures the microcontroller to resume activity when a critical event occurs.
- **Optimized Power Use**: Ensures the microcontroller only wakes up when necessary, saving power.

Syntax

```
set_wakeup_source(pin);
```

Syntax Explanation

- **pin**: The pin or source that will act as the wake-up trigger for the microcontroller.

Simple Code Example

```
set_wakeup_source(PIN2);
```

Code Example Explanation

- Configures PIN2 as a wake-up source so the microcontroller will exit sleep mode when this pin changes state.

Notes

- Different wake-up sources may be configured based on the microcontroller's capabilities.

Warnings

- Ensure the selected pin or event is suitable for your application to prevent unintended wake-ups.

---

3. Disable Peripheral (disable_peripheral)

What is Disable Peripheral?

The disable_peripheral function turns off a specific peripheral (like UART, ADC, or PWM) when it's not needed, conserving power by reducing active components.

Use Purpose

- **Reduce Unnecessary Power Usage**: Turns off components that are not actively used.
- **Optimize Efficiency**: Minimizes power consumption by focusing only on active peripherals.

Syntax

```
disable_peripheral(name);
```

Syntax Explanation

- **name**: The name of the peripheral to disable, such as UART, ADC, or PWM.

Simple Code Example

```
disable_peripheral(UART);
```

Code Example Explanation

- Disables the UART peripheral, saving power by turning off its circuitry.

Notes

- Re-enable peripherals before use.

Warnings

- Ensure the peripheral is not in use before disabling it, as this may cause operational issues.

---

4. Enable Peripheral (`enable_peripheral`)

What is Enable Peripheral?

The `enable_peripheral` function reactivates a specific peripheral that was previously turned off, allowing it to function again.

Use Purpose

- **Reactivate Peripherals as Needed**: Controls peripheral activation to manage power dynamically.
- **Selective Power Use**: Re-enables components based on application needs.

Syntax

```
enable_peripheral(name);
```

Syntax Explanation

- **name**: The peripheral to enable, such as UART, ADC, or PWM.

Simple Code Example

```
enable_peripheral(UART);
```

Code Example Explanation

- Enables the UART peripheral, allowing it to function after being disabled.

Notes

- Use enable/disable commands strategically to control power.

Warnings

- Enable peripherals only when necessary to avoid excessive power use.

---

5. Sleep for Duration (`sleep`)

What is Sleep for Duration?

The `sleep` function pauses the microcontroller for a specified time in milliseconds, saving power during inactive periods.

Use Purpose

- **Timed Power Reduction**: Temporarily reduces power usage for a fixed duration.
- **Simple Delay with Power Saving**: Ideal for non-critical delays in low-power applications.

Syntax

```
sleep(duration);
```

Syntax Explanation

- **duration**: The time, in milliseconds, for which the microcontroller should remain in low-power sleep mode.

Simple Code Example

```
sleep(500);  // Sleep for 500 ms
```

Code Example Explanation

- Puts the microcontroller in sleep mode for 500 milliseconds before resuming operations.

Notes

- Suitable for fixed delays where minimal power is used during waiting periods.

Warnings

- Ensure critical tasks are not delayed unintentionally by the sleep command.

Relevant Project Section

Project Name
Low-Power LED Control with Wake-Up on Button Press

Project Goal
Use power management functions on a RISC-V microcontroller to enter sleep mode and wake up on a button press. This project demonstrates the use of sleep modes and wake-up sources to control power usage effectively.

RISC-V Development Environment
This project will use **PlatformIO** in **Visual Studio Code**.

RISC-V Microcontroller
We will use the **SiFive HiFive1 Rev B** microcontroller for this project.

Requirement Components
- **SiFive HiFive1 Rev B Microcontroller**
- **LED** connected to a GPIO pin to indicate active state
- **Push Button** connected to a GPIO pin for wake-up

Component Connection Table

Component	RISC-V Pin	Additional Notes
LED	GPIO Pin 2	Indicates microcontroller activity
Button	GPIO Pin 3	Acts as a wake-up source from sleep mode

Connection Analysis

The LED is used to show the active state of the microcontroller, and the button serves as an external wake-up source. When the button is pressed, it wakes the microcontroller from sleep mode, and the LED turns on briefly to indicate activity.

Program Software Setup

1. Open **Visual Studio Code** and create a new PlatformIO project.
2. Set up the GPIO pins for the LED and the button.
3. Implement code to enter sleep mode, configure the button as a wake-up source, and control the LED.

Project Code

```
#include <stdint.h>
#include <stdio.h>

#define LED_PIN 2              // GPIO pin for LED
#define BUTTON_PIN 3           // GPIO pin for Button

void setup() {
    GPIO_DIR |= (1 << LED_PIN); // Set LED pin as output
    GPIO_DIR &= ~(1 << BUTTON_PIN); // Set button pin as input
    set_wakeup_source(BUTTON_PIN);   // Configure button as wake-up
source
}

void blinkLED() {
    GPIO_OUT |= (1 << LED_PIN);      // Turn LED on
    sleep(200);                      // Keep LED on for 200 ms
    GPIO_OUT &= ~(1 << LED_PIN);     // Turn LED off
}

int main() {
    setup();
```

```
    while (1) {
        enter_sleep_mode();   // Enter low-power mode
        blinkLED();           // Wake up and blink LED when button is
pressed
    }
}
```

Save and Run

1. Save, compile, and upload the code to the **SiFive HiFive1 Rev B** board using PlatformIO.
2. Observe the LED turning on briefly each time the button is pressed to wake the microcontroller.

Check Output

*   The LED should blink on for 200 ms each time the button is pressed, indicating the microcontroller woke from sleep.

Memory Management and EEPROM Usage in RISC-V Microcontrollers

Chapter Overview

Memory management in embedded systems involves allocating, storing, and accessing data efficiently to optimize performance and minimize memory usage. EEPROM (Electrically Erasable Programmable Read-Only Memory) is a type of non-volatile memory that allows microcontrollers to retain data even when powered off, making it ideal for storing configurations, calibration data, and persistent settings. This chapter covers essential memory management techniques, EEPROM usage, and a practical example on data storage and retrieval in RISC-V microcontrollers.

Chapter Goal

- Understand memory management concepts and how to use dynamic memory in embedded C programming.
- Learn to read and write data to EEPROM for persistent storage in embedded applications.
- Implement a project that saves settings to EEPROM and retrieves them after a reset.

Rules

- **Use Memory Efficiently**: Limit memory usage by minimizing dynamic allocations and using static memory wherever possible.
- **Store Persistent Data in EEPROM**: Use EEPROM for settings that need to persist across power cycles.
- **Limit EEPROM Writes**: EEPROM has a finite write cycle limit, so avoid frequent writes to prolong memory life.
- **Clear Unused Memory**: Release dynamically allocated memory after use to prevent memory leaks in applications with complex data handling.

Brief Introduction to Memory Management and EEPROM

Memory in embedded systems is often limited, so efficient memory allocation and usage are crucial. While dynamic memory allocation (malloc, free) allows flexible memory use, excessive or improper use can lead to fragmentation. EEPROM provides non-volatile storage, allowing data to be retained when the microcontroller is powered off, making it valuable for storing configuration parameters and calibration data that must persist.

Syntax Table

Serial No	Topic	Syntax	Simple Example
1	Dynamic Allocation	malloc(size);	int *ptr = malloc(10);
2	Free Memory	free(ptr);	free(ptr);
3	EEPROM Write	eeprom_write(addr, data);	eeprom_write(0x10, 45);
4	EEPROM Read	eeprom_read(addr);	int data = eeprom_read(0x10);
5	EEPROM Update	eeprom_update(addr, data);	eeprom_update(0x10, 45);

Detailed Breakdown for Each Command

1. Dynamic Allocation (malloc)

What is Dynamic Allocation?

malloc is used to allocate memory at runtime, which is essential in applications where the required memory size changes during execution. It returns a pointer to the beginning of the allocated memory.

Use Purpose

- **Flexible Memory Use**: Allows memory to be allocated as needed.
- **Data Buffers**: Useful for creating temporary buffers or data storage areas.

Syntax

```
malloc(size);
```

Syntax Explanation

- `size`: The amount of memory (in bytes) to allocate.

Simple Code Example

```
int *data = (int *)malloc(10 * sizeof(int));
```

Code Example Explanation

- Allocates memory for an array of 10 integers and assigns it to the pointer `data`.

Notes

- Always check if `malloc` returns NULL, which indicates allocation failure.

Warnings

- Forgetting to free allocated memory can lead to memory leaks, especially in large or complex programs.

---

2. Free Memory (`free`)

What is Free Memory?

The `free` function releases memory that was previously allocated with `malloc`, making it available for future allocations.

Use Purpose

- **Memory Cleanup**: Prevents memory leaks by releasing unused memory.
- **Efficient Memory Use**: Ensures memory is available for other parts of the program.

Syntax

```
free(ptr);
```

Syntax Explanation

- `ptr`: The pointer to the memory that needs to be freed.

Simple Code Example

```
free(data);
```

Code Example Explanation

- Frees the memory allocated to the `data` pointer, making it available for reuse.

Notes

- Only call `free` on memory allocated by `malloc`.

Warnings

- Avoid using `free` on memory that was not dynamically allocated, as this may cause undefined behavior.

---

3. EEPROM Write (eeprom_write)

What is EEPROM Write?

`eeprom_write` writes data to a specified EEPROM address, allowing data to be stored permanently across power cycles.

Use Purpose

- **Store Persistent Data**: Saves data that should be retained after a reset or power off.
- **Configuration Settings**: Useful for storing settings like thresholds or calibration values.

Syntax

```
eeprom_write(addr, data);
```

Syntax Explanation

- **addr**: The EEPROM address where data will be stored.
- **data**: The data to be written to the specified address.

Simple Code Example

```
eeprom_write(0x10, 45);
```

Code Example Explanation

- Writes the value 45 to EEPROM address 0x10.

Notes

- Writing to EEPROM is slower than regular memory access; use it sparingly.

Warnings

- EEPROM has a limited number of write cycles. Avoid frequent writes to prolong memory lifespan.

---

4. EEPROM Read (eeprom_read)

What is EEPROM Read?

eeprom_read retrieves data from a specified EEPROM address, allowing persistent data to be read back into the program.

Use Purpose

- **Retrieve Persistent Data**: Reads stored settings or parameters on startup.
- **Non-volatile Data Access**: Provides access to data that remains intact after power loss.

Syntax

```
eeprom_read(addr);
```

Syntax Explanation

- **addr**: The EEPROM address from which to read the data.

Simple Code Example
c
Copy code
```c
int value = eeprom_read(0x10);
```

Code Example Explanation

- Reads the value stored at EEPROM address 0x10 and stores it in `value`.

Notes

- Reading from EEPROM is slower than regular memory; use it only when necessary.

Warnings

- Avoid reading from uninitialized EEPROM addresses, as they may contain unpredictable values.

---

5. EEPROM Update (`eeprom_update`)

What is EEPROM Update?
`eeprom_update` checks if the data at the specified address already matches the new data before writing. This minimizes unnecessary writes, extending the EEPROM's life.

Use Purpose

- **Optimize EEPROM Writes**: Reduces wear on EEPROM by only writing data if it has changed.
- **Efficient Persistent Storage**: Maintains data integrity with minimal writes.

Syntax

```
eeprom_update(addr, data);
```

Syntax Explanation

- **addr**: The EEPROM address to be updated.
- **data**: The new data to be written if different from the current value.

Simple Code Example

```
eeprom_update(0x10, 45);
```

Code Example Explanation

- Updates EEPROM address 0x10 with the value 45 if it differs from the current stored value.

Notes

- eeprom_update is more efficient for high-write applications.

Warnings

- Use eeprom_update instead of eeprom_write when values may frequently change.

Relevant Project Section

Project Name
Settings Storage with EEPROM for a RISC-V Microcontroller

Project Goal
Use EEPROM and memory management functions to store and retrieve user-defined settings (e.g., a brightness level) on a RISC-V microcontroller. The settings persist even when the microcontroller is powered off, demonstrating effective EEPROM use.

RISC-V Development Environment
This project will use **PlatformIO** in **Visual Studio Code**.

RISC-V Microcontroller

We will use the **SiFive HiFive1 Rev B** microcontroller for this project.

Requirement Components

- **SiFive HiFive1 Rev B Microcontroller**
- **Push Button** to adjust settings
- **LED** connected to GPIO to display brightness level based on settings

Component Connection Table

Component	RISC-V Pin	Additional Notes
LED	GPIO Pin 2	Indicates brightness level
Push Button	GPIO Pin 3	Adjusts brightness level and stores in EEPROM

Connection Analysis

The push button is used to change the brightness level of the LED. The brightness level is saved to EEPROM and retrieved after a reset, allowing the system to remember the last setting. This project demonstrates how to write, read, and update values in EEPROM, along with dynamic memory handling.

Program Software Setup

1. Open **Visual Studio Code** and create a new PlatformIO project.
2. Configure GPIO pins for the LED and button.
3. Implement code to store and retrieve brightness level settings using EEPROM.

Project Code

```c
#include <stdint.h>
#include <stdio.h>

#define LED_PIN 2                // GPIO pin for LED
#define BUTTON_PIN 3             // GPIO pin for button
#define EEPROM_ADDR 0x10         // EEPROM address for brightness level
#define MAX_BRIGHTNESS 5

int brightness;

void setup() {
    GPIO_DIR |= (1 << LED_PIN);   // Set LED pin as output
    GPIO_DIR &= ~(1 << BUTTON_PIN); // Set button pin as input

    // Read stored brightness from EEPROM
    brightness = eeprom_read(EEPROM_ADDR);
    if (brightness > MAX_BRIGHTNESS || brightness < 0) {
        brightness = 0; // Set default if out of range
    }
}

void adjustBrightness() {
    // Increment brightness level
    brightness = (brightness + 1) % (MAX_BRIGHTNESS + 1);

    // Update EEPROM with new brightness level
    eeprom_update(EEPROM_ADDR, brightness);

    // Display brightness on LED (simple on/off based on brightness
level)
    if (brightness > 0) {
        GPIO_OUT |= (1 << LED_PIN);   // Turn LED on
    } else {
        GPIO_OUT &= ~(1 << LED_PIN); // Turn LED off
    }
}

int main() {
    setup();

    while (1) {
        // Check if button is pressed
        if (GPIO_IN & (1 << BUTTON_PIN)) {
            adjustBrightness();

            // Simple delay for button debounce
            for (volatile int i = 0; i < 100000; i++);
        }
    }
}
```

Save and Run

1. Save, compile, and upload the code to the **SiFive HiFive1 Rev B** board using PlatformIO.
2. Press the button to change the brightness level, and observe that the level persists after a reset.

Check Output

- The LED should turn on at different brightness levels each time the button is pressed, storing the setting in EEPROM. After a reset, the LED should return to the last brightness level.

Communication in RISC-V Microcontrollers

Chapter Overview

Communication in embedded systems allows microcontrollers to exchange data with other devices, sensors, or user interfaces. Common communication protocols include UART, SPI, and I2C, each serving specific types of applications with varying requirements for speed, data format, and connection topology. In this chapter, we'll explore the basics of these protocols and demonstrate communication with an external device using UART on a RISC-V microcontroller.

Chapter Goal

- Understand basic communication protocols for embedded systems, including UART, SPI, and I2C.
- Learn to set up and use UART communication on a RISC-V microcontroller.
- Implement a project that sends and receives data over UART to demonstrate communication functionality.

Rules

- **Choose the Right Protocol**: Use UART for simple serial communication, SPI for high-speed data transfer, and I2C for communication with multiple devices.
- **Configure Baud Rate Correctly**: Ensure both sender and receiver share the same baud rate for UART communication.
- **Use Proper Error Handling**: Implement checks for data integrity, such as parity bits or acknowledgments.
- **Monitor Communication Lines**: Ensure communication lines are free from interference, especially in noisy environments.

Brief Introduction to Communication Protocols

Embedded systems often need to communicate with other devices, such as sensors, displays, and other microcontrollers. UART (Universal Asynchronous Receiver/Transmitter) is a commonly used protocol that transmits data serially, ideal for simple, point-to-point connections. SPI (Serial Peripheral Interface) and I2C (Inter-Integrated Circuit) are more advanced protocols, supporting multiple devices and offering faster data transfer rates for complex systems.

Syntax Table

Serial No	Topic	Syntax	Simple Example
1	UART Initialization	`UART_INIT(baud_rate);`	`UART_INIT(9600);`
2	UART Transmit	`UART_WRITE(data);`	`UART_WRITE('A');`
3	UART Receive	`UART_READ();`	`char data = UART_READ();`
4	SPI Initialization	`SPI_INIT();`	`SPI_INIT();`
5	I2C Initialization	`I2C_INIT();`	`I2C_INIT();`

Detailed Breakdown for Each Command

1. UART Initialization (UART_INIT)

What is UART Initialization?

UART_INIT sets up the UART module with a specific baud rate, configuring the speed at which data is transmitted and received. Both communicating devices must share the same baud rate.

Use Purpose

- **Establish UART Communication**: Initializes UART to begin serial communication with external devices.
- **Set Baud Rate**: Defines the speed of communication, ensuring synchronization with other devices.

Syntax

```
UART_INIT(baud_rate);
```

Syntax Explanation

- **baud_rate**: The communication speed, typically in bits per second (bps), such as 9600 or 115200.

Simple Code Example

```
UART_INIT(9600);
```

Code Example Explanation

- Initializes UART with a baud rate of 9600 bps, configuring it for communication at this speed.

Notes

- Ensure the selected baud rate is compatible with the receiving device.

Warnings

- Mismatched baud rates will result in garbled or unreadable data.

---

2. UART Transmit (UART_WRITE)

What is UART Transmit?

UART_WRITE sends data over the UART line, typically one byte at a time. It's commonly used to transmit characters, numbers, or commands to other devices.

Use Purpose

- **Send Data**: Allows the microcontroller to send data to another UART-enabled device, such as a PC or sensor.
- **Control Communication**: Transmits commands or information to an external system.

Syntax

```
UART_WRITE(data);
```

Syntax Explanation

- **data**: The character or byte to be transmitted.

Simple Code Example

```
UART_WRITE('A');
```

Code Example Explanation

- Transmits the character 'A' over UART, sending it to the connected device.

Notes

- Multiple characters or strings may require looping through each character.

Warnings

- Ensure data is ready to be sent before calling UART_WRITE to avoid transmission issues.

---

3. UART Receive (UART_READ)

What is UART Receive?

UART_READ reads data received from another UART device, enabling the microcontroller to collect incoming information for processing.

Use Purpose

- **Receive Data**: Collects data sent from external devices for processing or storage.
- **Serial Data Logging**: Reads data from sensors or other microcontrollers.

Syntax

```
UART_READ();
```

Syntax Explanation

- Reads the incoming byte from the UART line.

Simple Code Example

```
char data = UART_READ();
```

Code Example Explanation

- Reads a byte from the UART line and stores it in the variable `data`.

Notes

- Use in combination with checks to ensure data is available before reading.

---

4. SPI Initialization (SPI_INIT)
What is SPI Initialization?

SPI_INIT initializes the SPI module for high-speed communication with SPI-compatible devices, such as displays and memory chips.

Use Purpose

- **Prepare SPI for Data Transfer**: Sets up SPI for communication with multiple devices at high speed.
- **Define Master/Slave Mode**: Configures the microcontroller as master or slave in the SPI communication.

Syntax

```
SPI_INIT();
```

Syntax Explanation

- No parameters are typically required; initializes SPI to default settings.

Simple Code Example

```
SPI_INIT();
```

Code Example Explanation

- Initializes the SPI module for communication with other SPI devices.

Notes

- Ensure that each SPI device has a unique chip select line.

Warnings

- Configure clock polarity and phase correctly to avoid data corruption.

---

5. I2C Initialization (I2C_INIT)

What is I2C Initialization?

I2C_INIT sets up the I2C bus for communication with I2C devices. I2C is a two-wire protocol, enabling multiple devices to communicate on the same bus with unique addresses.

Use Purpose

- **Prepare I2C for Multi-Device Communication**: Initializes the I2C bus for connecting multiple devices.
- **Define Master/Slave Roles**: Sets up the microcontroller as a master or slave in I2C communication.

Syntax

```
I2C_INIT();
```

Syntax Explanation

- Typically no parameters; initializes I2C with default settings.

Simple Code Example

```
I2C_INIT();
```

Code Example Explanation

- Initializes the I2C bus, enabling communication with multiple I2C devices.

Notes

- Each I2C device must have a unique address.

Warnings

- Incorrect address configurations may result in communication failure.

Relevant Project Section

Project Name
Serial Communication with Temperature Sensor

Project Goal
Use UART communication on a RISC-V microcontroller to send temperature readings from a sensor to a serial monitor. This project demonstrates the setup and use of UART to send data to an external device, allowing remote monitoring of sensor data.

RISC-V Development Environment
This project will use **PlatformIO** in **Visual Studio Code**.

RISC-V Microcontroller

We will use the **SiFive HiFive1 Rev B** microcontroller for this project.

Requirement Components

- **SiFive HiFive1 Rev B Microcontroller**
- **Analog Temperature Sensor** connected to an ADC pin
- **Serial Communication Interface** for data display on a terminal

Component Connection Table

Component	RISC-V Pin	Additional Notes
Temperature Sensor	ADC Pin	Analog temperature data input
Serial Interface	UART Pins	Displays temperature data in terminal

Connection Analysis

The temperature sensor provides an analog reading based on temperature. The microcontroller converts this to a digital value, processes it, and sends it over UART to a serial terminal, displaying temperature data in real-time.

Program Software Setup

1. Open **Visual Studio Code** and create a new PlatformIO project.
2. Set up the ADC for reading sensor data and configure UART for serial output.
3. Implement code to read temperature data, convert it, and transmit it via UART.

Project Code

```c
#include <stdint.h>
#include <stdio.h>

#define ADC_PIN 0                    // ADC channel for temperature sensor
#define BAUD_RATE 9600               // UART baud rate

void setup() {
    ADC_INIT();                      // Initialize ADC
    UART_INIT(BAUD_RATE);            // Initialize UART for serial output
}

// Function to read and convert temperature data
float readTemperature() {
    int adcValue = ADC_READ();                    // Read ADC value
    float voltage = (adcValue / 1023.0) * 3.3;    // Convert to voltage
    return voltage * 100;                         // Convert voltage to
temperature
}

void sendTemperature(float temperature) {
    char buffer[20];
    sprintf(buffer, "Temp: %.2f°C\n", temperature);

    for (int i = 0; buffer[i] != '\0'; i++) {
        UART_WRITE(buffer[i]);   // Send each character over UART
    }
}

int main() {
    setup();

    while (1) {
        float temperature = readTemperature();   // Read temperature
from sensor
        sendTemperature(temperature);            // Send temperature
over UART

        for (volatile int i = 0; i < 1000000; i++);   // Simple delay
    }
}
```

Save and Run

1. Save, compile, and upload the code to the **SiFive HiFive1 Rev B** board using PlatformIO.
2. Open a serial monitor in PlatformIO set to 9600 baud to observe the temperature data.

Check Output

- The serial monitor should display temperature readings in Celsius, sent periodically from the microcontroller.

Debugging and Testing in RISC-V Microcontrollers

Chapter Overview
Debugging and testing are crucial for identifying and fixing issues in embedded programs, ensuring code reliability and performance. Effective debugging techniques allow developers to trace issues, understand code behavior, and verify system functionality. Testing involves systematically checking code behavior, verifying correctness, and ensuring the system meets design requirements. In this chapter, we will cover common debugging tools, techniques, and testing strategies for RISC-V microcontrollers.

Chapter Goal

- Understand debugging tools and techniques available for RISC-V microcontrollers.
- Learn how to set breakpoints, step through code, and use serial debugging.
- Implement a project that demonstrates debugging by testing a temperature sensor's data output and analyzing issues.

Rules

- **Use Breakpoints for Step-by-Step Debugging**: Breakpoints allow code inspection without interrupting the entire program.
- **Implement Serial Debugging Messages**: Use serial output to check variable values and system states.
- **Verify Code Logic with Unit Tests**: For critical functions, create small test cases to confirm correct functionality.
- **Record Test Results and Issues**: Maintain a log of errors and solutions to improve future debugging and development processes.

Brief Introduction to Debugging and Testing

Debugging in embedded systems involves using tools to identify and fix errors in code. Serial debugging, breakpoints, and watches help track variable states and execution flow. Testing involves running the program under different conditions to check for bugs or logical errors. Testing techniques, such as unit testing and functional testing, help ensure that each part of the system performs as expected.

Syntax Table

Serial No	Topic	Syntax	Simple Example
1	Serial Print Debugging	`printf("message");`	`printf("Value: %d\n", val);`
2	Breakpoint	`// Set breakpoint here`	`// Debug here`
3	Watch Variable	`watch variable_name;`	`watch counter;`
4	Step Over	`step_over();`	`step_over();`
5	Unit Test Function	`void test_function();`	`void test_addition();`

Detailed Breakdown for Each Command
1. Serial Print Debugging (`printf`)

What is Serial Print Debugging?
Serial print debugging involves sending messages or variable values over the serial interface, allowing developers to observe code execution and inspect values in real-time.

Use Purpose

- **Monitor Variable Values**: Provides visibility into variable states during runtime.
- **Track Program Flow**: Helps in understanding the sequence of code execution.

Syntax

```
printf("message");
```

Syntax Explanation

- **"message"**: The text or variable to be displayed on the serial monitor.

Simple Code Example

```
int value = 10;
printf("Value: %d\n", value);
```

Code Example Explanation

- Sends the message Value: 10 to the serial monitor, displaying the variable value.

Notes

- Use \n for a new line in the serial output to improve readability.

Warnings

- Excessive print statements may slow down the program; use them selectively.

---

2. Breakpoint
What is a Breakpoint?

A breakpoint is a marker in code where execution pauses, allowing developers to inspect variable states and code behavior at a specific point.

Use Purpose

- **Pause Execution**: Stops the program to allow code inspection.
- **Analyze Code Flow**: Identifies which parts of the code execute and helps locate errors.

Syntax

```
// Set breakpoint here
```

Syntax Explanation

- **// Set breakpoint here**: Placeholder indicating where to place a breakpoint in debugging software.

Simple Code Example

```
int counter = 0;  // Set breakpoint here
counter++;
```

Code Example Explanation

- Sets a breakpoint on counter = 0;, pausing execution before counter is incremented.

Notes

- Breakpoints are set in the IDE/debugging tool, not directly in code.

Warnings

- Ensure breakpoints are removed in final production code to prevent interruptions.

---

3. Watch Variable

What is Watch Variable?
A watch allows developers to monitor specific variables as the program executes, helping to track changes in value.

Use Purpose

- **Track Variable Changes**: Observes how a variable's value changes throughout the program.
- **Identify Logic Errors**: Detects unexpected changes that may indicate bugs.

Syntax

```
watch variable_name;
```

Syntax Explanation

- **`variable_name`**: The variable being monitored.

Simple Code Example

```
int temperature = 25;  // Watch temperature
temperature += 5;
```

Code Example Explanation

- Sets a watch on `temperature`, tracking its value as it changes.

Notes

- Watches are often set up in debugging software, not directly in the code.

Warnings

- Watches can slow down debugging in complex programs; use only essential variables.

---

4. Step Over (`step_over`)

What is Step Over?
Step Over is a debugging command that allows developers to execute one line of code at a time without entering functions, useful for observing execution without diving into each function.

Use Purpose

- **Inspect Code Line-by-Line**: Allows precise control over code execution for detailed analysis.
- **Skip Function Details**: Executes functions without entering them, useful for large or well-tested functions.

Syntax

```
step_over();
```

Syntax Explanation

- No parameters; simply advances code execution to the next line.

Simple Code Example

```
int result = add(3, 5);  // Step over this line
```

Code Example Explanation

- Steps over the add function call, executing it without entering the function.

Notes

- Step Over is used in debugging software rather than directly in code.

Warnings

- Use with discretion; complex function calls may require stepping into for detailed debugging.

---

5. Unit Test Function (`void test_function`)

What is Unit Test Function?
A unit test function verifies the correctness of a specific function or code segment by running predefined test cases.

Use Purpose

- **Validate Function Logic**: Ensures each function performs as expected with known inputs.
- **Detect Early Errors**: Helps catch issues before integrating functions into larger systems.

Syntax

```
void test_function();
```

Syntax Explanation

- **test_function**: A self-contained function created for testing other functions.

Simple Code Example

```c
void test_addition() {
    int result = add(3, 5);
    if (result == 8) {
        printf("Test Passed\n");
    } else {
        printf("Test Failed\n");
    }
}
```

Code Example Explanation

- Tests the add function by checking if the result of add(3, 5) is 8.

Notes

- Unit tests should cover edge cases to ensure robustness.

Warnings

- Ensure test cases are independent and do not rely on other tests to function correctly.

Relevant Project Section

Project Name
Debugging a Temperature Monitoring System

Project Goal
Use debugging techniques to test and verify the accuracy of a temperature monitoring system on a RISC-V microcontroller. This project demonstrates using serial print statements, breakpoints, and unit tests to troubleshoot and ensure reliable functionality.

RISC-V Development Environment
This project will use **PlatformIO** in **Visual Studio Code**.

RISC-V Microcontroller
We will use the **SiFive HiFive1 Rev B** microcontroller for this project.

Requirement Components

- **SiFive HiFive1 Rev B Microcontroller**
- **Analog Temperature Sensor** connected to an ADC pin
- **Serial Monitor** to display debug messages and values

Component Connection Table

Component	RISC-V Pin	Additional Notes
Temperature Sensor	ADC Pin	Analog temperature data input
Serial Interface	UART Pins	Displays debug output in terminal

Connection Analysis
The temperature sensor provides an analog reading based on temperature. The microcontroller reads and processes this data, using serial debugging to display values and verify system performance.

Program Software Setup

1. Open **Visual Studio Code** and create a new PlatformIO project.
2. Set up the ADC for reading sensor data and configure UART for serial output.
3. Implement code to read temperature data, test values, and use debugging techniques to check for accuracy.

Project Code

```c
#include <stdint.h>
#include <stdio.h>

#define ADC_PIN 0              // ADC channel for temperature sensor
#define BAUD_RATE 9600         // UART baud rate
#define TEMP_THRESHOLD 25      // Example temperature threshold for
testing

void setup() {
    ADC_INIT();                // Initialize ADC
    UART_INIT(BAUD_RATE);      // Initialize UART for serial output
}

// Function to read and convert temperature data
float readTemperature() {
    int adcValue = ADC_READ();                  // Read ADC value
    float voltage = (adcValue / 1023.0) * 3.3;  // Convert to voltage
    return voltage * 100;                       // Convert voltage to
temperature
}

// Test function to verify temperature calculations
void testTemperatureConversion() {
    float temp = readTemperature();
    printf("Debug - Temperature: %.2f°C\n", temp);
    if (temp >= TEMP_THRESHOLD) {
        printf("Temperature is above threshold.\n");
    } else {
        printf("Temperature is below threshold.\n");
    }
}
int main() {
    setup();

    // Set a breakpoint here for debugging
    while (1) {
        float temperature = readTemperature();  // Read temperature
from sensor
        testTemperatureConversion();            // Run test for
debugging

        for (volatile int i = 0; i < 1000000; i++);  // Simple delay
    }
}
```

Save and Run

1. Save, compile, and upload the code to the **SiFive HiFive1 Rev B** board using PlatformIO.
2. Open a serial monitor in PlatformIO set to 9600 baud to observe the temperature data and debug messages.

Check Output

- The serial monitor should display temperature readings and messages indicating whether the temperature is above or below the threshold. Use breakpoints and watch variables to monitor `temperature` during testing.

Wi-Fi IoT Applications in RISC-V Microcontrollers

Chapter Overview
Wi-Fi-enabled IoT applications allow devices to connect to the internet, enabling remote data transmission, control, and monitoring. RISC-V microcontrollers with Wi-Fi capabilities, or through external Wi-Fi modules, can be integrated into IoT systems for a variety of applications, from sensor data monitoring to remote device control. This chapter covers the basics of Wi-Fi communication, including setting up a Wi-Fi connection, sending data to a cloud server, and receiving commands from a remote device.

Chapter Goal
- Understand the process of setting up Wi-Fi communication on a RISC-V microcontroller.
- Learn to connect to a Wi-Fi network and send data to a server or cloud platform.
- Implement a project to monitor sensor data and transmit it over Wi-Fi for IoT applications.

Rules
- **Ensure Network Security**: Use encryption (WPA2) and secure protocols for data transfer to protect IoT data.
- **Monitor Connection Status**: Implement checks to detect disconnection and reconnect if needed.
- **Optimize Data Transmission**: Send data only when necessary to reduce network congestion and save power.
- **Use APIs for Cloud Communication**: Follow the API specifications of cloud platforms for reliable data exchange.

Brief Introduction to Wi-Fi in IoT Applications
Wi-Fi communication in IoT devices allows data to be sent to and received from remote servers. With Wi-Fi, embedded devices can push sensor data to the cloud, receive commands, and enable remote monitoring and control. This functionality expands applications, from smart homes to industrial automation. Common protocols used in IoT Wi-Fi communication include HTTP for web-based applications and MQTT for lightweight, efficient data exchange.

Syntax Table

Serial No	Topic	Syntax	Simple Example
1	Wi-Fi Initialization	`wifi_init(ssid, password);`	`wifi_init("MySSID", "password");`
2	Connect to Network	`wifi_connect();`	`wifi_connect();`
3	Send Data Over HTTP	`http_post(url, data);`	`http_post("http://server", data);`
4	Receive Data Over HTTP	`http_get(url);`	`http_get("http://server");`
5	Wi-Fi Disconnect	`wifi_disconnect();`	`wifi_disconnect();`

Detailed Breakdown for Each Command

1. Wi-Fi Initialization (`wifi_init`)

What is Wi-Fi Initialization?

The `wifi_init` function initializes Wi-Fi settings, specifying the network SSID (name) and password to allow the device to connect securely to a Wi-Fi network.

Use Purpose

- **Set Wi-Fi Credentials**: Configures the Wi-Fi module with network credentials.
- **Enable Internet Access**: Prepares the device to communicate over Wi-Fi.

Syntax

```
wifi_init(ssid, password);
```

Syntax Explanation

- **ssid**: The name of the Wi-Fi network.
- **password**: The Wi-Fi network password for secure access.

Simple Code Example

```
wifi_init("MyWiFiNetwork", "mysecurepassword");
```

Code Example Explanation

- Initializes Wi-Fi with the network name "MyWiFiNetwork" and the password "mysecurepassword".

Notes

- Ensure that the SSID and password are correct for successful connection.

Warnings

- Avoid hardcoding passwords in production code; use secure methods for handling credentials.

---

2. Connect to Network (`wifi_connect`)

What is Connect to Network?

The `wifi_connect` function connects the microcontroller to the specified Wi-Fi network, making it accessible for internet communication.

Use Purpose

- **Establish Network Connection**: Initiates the connection to enable data exchange with external servers or devices.
- **Enable IoT Communication**: Allows the microcontroller to send and receive data over the internet.

Syntax

```
wifi_connect();
```

Syntax Explanation

- No parameters; attempts to connect to the Wi-Fi network using the initialized SSID and password.

Simple Code Example

```
wifi_connect();
```

Code Example Explanation

- Connects the microcontroller to the Wi-Fi network previously set up with `wifi_init`.

Notes

- It is good practice to check the connection status to ensure successful connection.

Warnings

- Reconnection logic may be needed to handle intermittent connections.

---

3. Send Data Over HTTP (`http_post`)

What is Send Data Over HTTP?

The `http_post` function sends data to a specified server URL using the HTTP POST method, commonly used for uploading data in IoT applications.

Use Purpose

- **Upload Data to Cloud**: Sends sensor readings or other data to a server.
- **Control Remote Actions**: Sends commands to a cloud-based application or web service.

Syntax

```
http_post(url, data);
```

Syntax Explanation

- **url**: The server endpoint for data posting.
- **data**: The data payload to send, often in JSON format for IoT.

Simple Code Example

```
http_post("http://example.com/api/upload", "{\"temp\": 25}");
```

Code Example Explanation

- Posts temperature data to the specified URL as a JSON string.

Notes

- The server should be configured to receive and handle HTTP POST requests.

Warnings

- Ensure the URL is correct and the server can process HTTP POST requests.

---

4. Receive Data Over HTTP (http_get)
What is Receive Data Over HTTP?

The http_get function retrieves data from a specified server URL using the HTTP GET method, often used to pull settings or commands from a server.

Use Purpose

- **Retrieve Remote Data**: Fetches information, such as configuration settings or commands.
- **Enable Cloud-Based Control**: Retrieves data for controlling IoT devices remotely.

Syntax

```
http_get(url);
```

Syntax Explanation

- **url**: The server endpoint from which to retrieve data.

Simple Code Example

```
char response = http_get("http://example.com/api/settings");
```

Code Example Explanation

- Fetches settings data from the specified URL, storing it in response.

Notes

- Ensure the endpoint is accessible and configured to handle GET requests.

Warnings

- Excessive GET requests can increase bandwidth usage; use only as needed.

---

5. Wi-Fi Disconnect (`wifi_disconnect`)

What is Wi-Fi Disconnect?

wifi_disconnect ends the Wi-Fi connection, putting the device offline, which can save power and improve security when the connection is no longer needed.

Use Purpose

- **Save Power**: Disconnects from the network to reduce power consumption.
- **Enhance Security**: Prevents unwanted access when network access is not required.

Syntax

```
wifi_disconnect();
```

Syntax Explanation

- No parameters; disconnects the device from the Wi-Fi network.

Simple Code Example

```
wifi_disconnect();
```

Code Example Explanation

- Disconnects from the Wi-Fi network, stopping all internet communication.

Notes

- Ensure all required data transfers are complete before disconnecting.

Warnings

- Reconnecting after a disconnect may require reinitialization in some systems.

Relevant Project Section

Project Name
Wi-Fi Temperature Monitoring System

Project Goal
Use Wi-Fi communication on a RISC-V microcontroller to monitor temperature data from a sensor and transmit it to a cloud server. This project demonstrates setting up Wi-Fi, connecting to a network, and sending data to a server for remote monitoring.

RISC-V Development Environment
This project will use **PlatformIO** in **Visual Studio Code**.

RISC-V Microcontroller

We will use the **SiFive HiFive1 Rev B** microcontroller, with an external Wi-Fi module connected via UART.

Requirement Components

- **SiFive HiFive1 Rev B Microcontroller**
- **Wi-Fi Module** connected via UART
- **Analog Temperature Sensor** connected to an ADC pin
- **Cloud Server Endpoint** for receiving data

Component Connection Table

Component	RISC-V Pin	Additional Notes
Wi-Fi Module	UART Pins	Connects to Wi-Fi for cloud data upload
Temperature Sensor	ADC Pin	Provides analog temperature data

Connection Analysis

The Wi-Fi module is configured for internet access via a specified SSID and password. Temperature data from the sensor is read and then uploaded periodically to a cloud server, enabling remote monitoring.

Program Software Setup

1. Open **Visual Studio Code** and create a new PlatformIO project.
2. Configure the UART interface for Wi-Fi communication and ADC for temperature data.
3. Implement code to initialize Wi-Fi, read temperature data, and send it to a cloud server.

Project Code

```c
#include <stdint.h>
#include <stdio.h>

#define ADC_PIN 0              // ADC channel for temperature sensor
#define SSID "MyWiFiNetwork"   // Wi-Fi SSID
#define PASSWORD "mypassword"  // Wi-Fi password
#define SERVER_URL "http://example.com/api/upload"

void setup() {
    ADC_INIT();                 // Initialize ADC
    wifi_init(SSID, PASSWORD);   // Initialize Wi-Fi with network
credentials
    wifi_connect();             // Connect to Wi-Fi network
}

// Function to read and convert temperature data
float readTemperature() {
    int adcValue = ADC_READ();                     // Read ADC value
    float voltage = (adcValue / 1023.0) * 3.3;  // Convert to voltage
    return voltage * 100;                          // Convert voltage to
temperature
}

// Function to send temperature data to server
void sendTemperature(float temperature) {
    char data[50];
    sprintf(data, "{\"temperature\": %.2f}", temperature);
    http_post(SERVER_URL, data);
}

int main() {
    setup();

    while (1) {
        float temperature = readTemperature();  // Read temperature
from sensor
        sendTemperature(temperature);              // Send temperature
over Wi-Fi

        for (volatile int i = 0; i < 1000000; i++);  // Simple delay
for testing
    }
}
```

Save and Run

1. Save, compile, and upload the code to the **SiFive HiFive1 Rev B** board using PlatformIO.
2. Monitor the server to see temperature data updates.

Check Output

- Verify that the temperature data is uploaded to the server as JSON, showing up periodically in the specified endpoint.

www.ingramcontent.com/pod-product-compliance
Lightning Source LLC
LaVergne TN
LVHW051322050326
832903LV00031B/3322